At David C Cook, we equip the local church around the corner and around the globe to make disciples. Come see how we are working together—go to **www.davidccook.com**. Thank you!

transforming lives together

What people are saying about …

SelfLess

"Megan is one of my favorite people. She's a master storyteller, and if you've not had the chance to be in a room when she's speaking, fix that in a hurry. And bring a seatbelt. Here's why—she's real, she's full of joy, and she doesn't make everything about her. This book is a beautiful reminder that next to grace, one of God's best ideas was making you."

—**Bob Goff**, *New York Times* bestselling author of *Love Does*

"Megan lives and writes from a place of sincerity and passion that is contagious. When she writes, we should read. When she speaks, we should listen. *SelfLess* is a must read."

—**Brady Boyd**, pastor of New Life Church, Colorado Springs; author of *Addicted to Busy* and *Speak Life*

"Megan lives one of the most inspiring lives of any person I know. Reading *SelfLess*, it was clear this is her personal manifesto, how she understands God and orients her daily life around God's story. The words on these pages will draw you in and let you understand what your life can be in God."

—**Steve Carter**, teaching pastor of Willow Creek Community Church, South Barrington, IL; author of *This Invitational Life*

"In *SelfLess*, Megan Marshman gives a refreshing and honest perspective to the freedom the gospel offers. Her compelling storytelling and engaging illustrations allow the reader to participate in the journey of seeing life as something more than our small plot lines or trying to somehow earn a better part with good behavior or trying harder. Weaving together both vulnerability and strength on every page, Megan beckons those who are willing to become part of a story that is bigger than they could ever imagine … God's!"

—**Michelle Anthony**, executive pastor of families, New Life Church, Colorado Springs; author of *Spiritual Parenting, Becoming a Spiritually Healthy Family*, and *7 Family Ministry Essentials*

"Megan's insight to our identity in Christ comes from a relatable, honest, and unique perspective. She has a way of demystifying complex concepts and turning them into empowering, life-giving, and biblically based principles. This book shows that choosing to become *SelfLess* is the path to discovering your true self, as God originally intended."

—**David Martin**, speaker, pastor of Desperation Student Ministries, New Life Church, Colorado Springs

"*SelfLess* is a refreshing look at life, purpose, and being filled up with God. Megan delivers a passionate and biblical look at how we can get out of the way so God can have His way in our lives."

—**Debbie Alsdorf**, author of *The Faith Dare*, founder Design4LivingMinistries

"Megan becomes honest and vulnerable in this book to point us away from ourselves and toward the One who is actually the main character of life: Jesus. Her perspectives are refreshing. Her vulnerability brings hope, reminding each of us that we all are in process. But her desire to make much of Jesus, and to introduce us to the life and purpose that He invites us to, is compelling whether you've been walking with Jesus for a while or are just starting to think about it. This book is a quick read but it is not simple. It is challenging, filled with truth while drowned in grace, challenging us toward true selflessness."

—**Brian Holland**, teaching and campus
pastor, Purpose Church, Pomona, CA

"Megan had me at page 2. While she talks about the fallacy of tilting one's cup toward empty sources, the pages read like a mirror and stir the emptiness of one's soul. A bold and yet graceful challenge for all of us on how to be selfless."

—**Ron Hunter Jr.**, Ph.D., CEO of Randall
House and D6 Ministries, author of *The DNA of
D6: Building Blocks of Generational Discipleship*

"Megan is almost as fun in print as she is when she speaks. Almost. But that is more than okay. An almost with Megan is not like an almost with anyone else. She is such an extraordinarily skilled communicator—skilled in ways that cannot be taught— that her giftedness and voice come through even in print. *SelfLess* sets forth the gospel as winsomely and compellingly as I have ever heard it proclaimed. When I finished it, I wanted to give my heart to Jesus all over again. And I did, with tears. Really. Thanks, Megan."

—**Ben Patterson**, author of several books;
campus pastor, Westmont College

"I came to this book nearly out of breath. I was tired and overwhelmed by all that life brings and all that my heart—with its episodes of guilt, shame, and fear—demands. But within the pages of this book I found freedom and a renewed sense of how good the *good news* really is. Whether or not you believe it, buy into it, or live like it, God loves you, and that love changes everything."

—**Nick Benoit**, creative director
at Willow Creek Community
Church, South Barrington, IL

"*SelfLess* is a timeless reminder of who we are and get to be. God invites us into His story, to live out a life of freedom, to commune with Him through the grace given through Jesus Christ. Far too often, we rely upon the accolades of people we deem important or upon our social media status to declare our worth without truly being known. God has given us His Son, Jesus Christ, to fill us so that we can be contagious participants in His love story. Megan Fate Marshman writes from the heart using poignant examples from day-to-day life, ushering us back to God's truth and the joy that abounds as a result of living selfless."

—**Chris Simning**, national and
international speaker

"Megan Fate Marshman is the up-and-coming communicator of this generation, an author and speaker to follow. With a passion to challenge this current generation, she directly confronts our innate need to find love anywhere other than God Himself. If you are looking for a way to stop chasing the wrong things and feel the love the Creator wants for you, *SelfLess* is the book to read."

—**Evan Liewer**, senior director of program
ministries at Forest Home Camps

"The power of words can change our trajectory. Through Megan's winsome storytelling, God will use the letters on these pages to launch you into a new chapter of selfless living."

—**Brian Wurzell**, worship pastor, Hillside
Community Church, Rancho Cucamonga, CA

"In *SelfLess*, Megan humbly and poignantly helps us reorient our lives—our "cups"—in the right direction, showing us how to live in and out of the abundance and overflow of the gospel. Story-driven and personal, I recommend this book to anyone who wants deep faith and a purpose-filled life."

—**Jessie Minassian**, blogger at LifeLoveandGod.
com, author of *Unashamed and Family: How
to Love Yours (and Help Them Like You Back)*

"At a time in the world when too many people are looking to fill their cups in all the wrong ways, this little gem of a book has come to bring a fresh and much-needed perspective. Megan's thoughts and reflections will be immediately transferable to the life of any reader. It's time for many of us to recapture a biblical perspective of our true value through the lens of our Creator. *SelfLess* is here to get us on our way!"

—**Brent Eldridge**, lead pastor, Arbor
Road Church, Long Beach, CA;
chaplain for the LA Galaxy

"I have known Megan for over ten years, and in that time it has been a privilege to watch her grow in her knowledge and passion for the Lord. This idea of selfless living has been something God has been teaching her over the last few years, and I am very excited she has put these thoughts and ideas into a book. The way she simplifies this complicated topic of selfless living, as well as how she connects these ideas to today's culture, is truly is a gift. I am so proud of my friend."

—**Rich Baker**, pastor of communities at
Arbor Road Church, Long Beach, CA

SelfLess

LIVING YOUR PART IN THE BIG STORY OF GOD

MEGAN FATE MARSHMAN

David C Cook

transforming lives together

SELFLESS
Published by David C Cook
4050 Lee Vance Drive
Colorado Springs, CO 80918 U.S.A.

David C Cook U.K., Kingsway Communications
Eastbourne, East Sussex BN23 6NT, England

The graphic circle C logo is a registered trademark of David C Cook.

LCCN 2017945209
ISBN 978-1-4347-1230-1
eISBN 978-8-4347-1231-8

The Team: Alice Crider, Jeff Gerke, Amy Konyndyk, Rachael
Stevenson, Diane Gardner, Susan Murdock
Cover Design: Nick Lee
Cover Photo: Getty Images

Printed in the United States of America
First Edition 2017

2 3 4 5 6 7 8 9 10 11

080117

To my son, Foster.

Your father and I love you deeply.

"For God has not given us a spirit of fear and timidity, but of power, love, and self-discipline."
—2 Timothy 1:7 (NLT)

Contents

Acknowledgments

I would like to thank …

My husband, Randy. You promised my dad you would never hold me back. Thank you for keeping that promise. This book wouldn't be in existence if you hadn't encouraged me to do more than I could have ever dreamed of.

My mom, for being a living example of what selfless means; my dad, who's always been who I've wanted to become; my sister, Kimi, for being my biggest fan and living in such a way that I've become yours; and Dan and Shirley, whose intentional support is never-ending.

My partner in ministry who I look up to as a pioneer, Michelle Anthony. Thank you for believing in me and for modeling leadership and obedience to discern and share God's voice.

My community of faith for passionately pursuing God with me.

The team at David C Cook (specifically Verne, Alice, Matt, Chriscynethia, Michele, Byron, Dave, Annette, Rachael, Diane,

Susan, and Nick) for their partnership and commitment to equip the church with Christ-centered resources for making and teaching disciples who obediently transform today's generations.

Jeff Gerke, words may never express my gratitude for your professional advice, talent, passion, gifts, and assistance in creating this manuscript.

Introduction

Running on Empty

I have a cup.

My cup is metaphorical. It holds love. Love for others, love for myself.

You have a cup too.

Growing up, I ran around and splashed love on everyone with my cup of love. I've always loved loving people.

The only problem with my cup was that, after I loved someone, I held out my now-empty cup in their direction to be filled by their opinions of me. When people liked me, I *felt* filled up. I was filling my cup with their splashes of good opinions, and I thought that would satisfy me. If they liked me, appreciated me, noticed me, or pursued me, then I *felt* filled up.

And it worked, for a bit … just enough to keep me coming back for more.

But I discovered a problem: What happens when they don't notice you? When they don't appreciate your efforts? When you discover you're holding out your empty cups in the direction of people who are holding out their empty cup in your direction?

For me, holding my cup outward didn't stop in childhood. It crept into my marriage, and eventually I found myself holding out my cup to be filled by my son. As you might guess (or might know), all that running around only made me emptier.

Maybe you understand this running around very well. Maybe people ask you how you are and you answer "Good" or "Fine" even though you're really not okay. You're empty.

I know many people like this. As I write this, I think of one friend in particular who tries to convince herself, with the love from her cup, that she is good enough. That she has what it takes and is worth something. That she is worthy of using up oxygen and taking up space.

Since she was little, she's had this fear that maybe she wasn't worthy of love. Other people were okay, but not her. Her … she was only provisionally, temporarily approved for life. So long as she pleased people and achieved impressive things, she believed she had the right to exist. But when she failed at something or when it had been a long time since she'd done anything praiseworthy, she started to worry. Like really worry.

Now, the whole time she didn't know she had this metaphorical cup I'm talking about. That awareness came much later. All she knew was that sometimes she felt okay, but not nearly enough of the time. Most often, she felt either not-okay or just-about-to-be-not-okay. She spent that upsetting time trying to get back to feeling merely okay.

She felt like her cup, even if she didn't think of it as a cup, had somehow leaked everything out, and if she couldn't get it filled fast she didn't know what would happen, but she knew it would be bad. She needed her life passport renewed, like yesterday, and the only way she could think of to do it was to *trade* love with people.

This girl grew up in church, so she'd always known that God is love. She'd always known He wants us to shower love on other people. So feeling like she was being completely focused on others— and not realizing at all that she was doing it mainly to earn payback for herself—she'd pour some of her own love in the cup and splash people with it. She'd hug someone, so they'd *feel* her love. She'd serve someone, so they'd *see* her love. She'd volunteer at the church, so people would *know* her love's expanse. Splash, splash, splash—love, love, love.

And then, after showering her love onto others, she'd hold her empty cup out to them and just wait. Hoping. Eager. "*Please fill my cup in return!* I gave, now you have to give back. That's the rule. I need you to notice me, appreciate me, accept me. Please pour into my life the approval I need. Tomorrow, we can do it all again. But please, I'm so thirsty. Please love me!"

Sometimes, it worked. People would love her back. And then she felt great … for a little while. Or she'd succeed or win or achieve, and people would praise her … for a day. If she was the best—or at least *better than*—she felt filled. If she was impressive or had more social media followers than someone else or got some honor, she felt she'd outrun the empty-cup inspector for one more twenty-four-hour period and she could go on, slightly relaxed, and gear up to try impressing people again tomorrow.

By the way, it's okay to enjoy being social. We shouldn't care about having more followers than someone else just to try to feel like good people, but we *should* all just enjoy being social.

That constant, daily, never-ending chore of refilling the cup exhausted her.

Plus, sometimes she couldn't get anyone to fill her stupid cup. Sometimes her friends weren't her friends. Sometimes she didn't earn people's attention or win the game or get the award. Sometimes someone else got more followers than she had. Sometimes her family let her down. Sometimes she let *herself* down.

Sometimes everything shattered. Everything failed. All her attempts fell short. And she'd be left staring at an empty, bone-dry cup, wondering how she was going to get through one more day.

Here's the kicker: sometimes she looked around at the people she was asking to fill her cup, and she saw that *they were all holding their empty cups out to her.*

KNOW WHAT I MEAN?

Is this your life? Are you running around doing way too much while simultaneously feeling as though you're not doing enough? There has to be more, doesn't there?

All of us are born with a desire to be filled, truly satisfied, and whole. Each of us really does have a cup, and it really does need to be filled.

The question is, how can it be filled? And is there a way for it to stay *permanently* filled?

The answer to the second question is yes, there is a way for it to stay full forever. What fills it doesn't have to leak out. (We'll get back to the question of how later.)

Think about how a cup is designed to be used. You don't fill a cup and then lay it on its side and expect it to hold anything but air, right? A cup ends up on its side only by accident or when it's being cleaned or put away. Normally, you set a cup on a flat surface on its bottom, causing the opening to face up.

To be filled, your cup has to face upward toward God for Him to fill. Eventually, it will become so full you won't be able to contain the love that spills out to everyone else.

That's a picture of the Christian life lived the right way. That's what lies in your future.

The Christian life is an overflow of a full cup, not a constant effort to fill a cup that's forever leaking. When we tilt our cups upward and trust God to do His part, we can stop running around to people, hoping they will fill us.

Be assured that the Lord Jesus Christ wants you and me to be, as Paul wrote, "filled to the measure of all the fullness of God" (Eph. 3:19).

This type of life is not only possible; it's the best possible life. And it's yours for the asking.

MY ADULT-SIZED CUP

As I mentioned earlier, for me, holding my cup outward for others to fill didn't stop in childhood. It crept into all my friendships. It invaded my marriage. And eventually, tragically, I found myself holding out my cup to be filled by my son.

The form this pathetic cup-tilting took when I became an adult was mainly comparison and unhealthy expectations. Could I get more people to follow me online? Could I gain some award or marker of appreciation at work? Could I outdo others in a variety of categories: owning cool toys, a fancy car, or a beautiful house, or even in the number of friends I have? The list embarrassingly goes on.

Worse, I started comparing *children*. How many months would it take my son to roll over? Why wouldn't he crawl? The other kids were already crawling! Come on, kid, say, "Mama," quick! But wait until I've got my camera ready so I can post my—I mean, *your*—achievement online.

I hadn't realized I was pitting my child in a race against other children until one day when I saw a boy the same age as my son (nine months) take his first steps. I knew I should be excited for him and his mom, but I found myself feeling disappointed. *Less than,* somehow. Overshadowed and underworthy.

Cue my competitive side. I vowed to get my boy walking before any more little, um, darlings could pass him up.

I kept standing him up. He kept smiling and then plopping right back down. *Gah!* Back on your feet, kid.

Smile. *Plop.*

My son's first birthday came and went and he *still* wasn't walking.

As I reflect back now on my first year of motherhood, I begin to understand Theodore Roosevelt's words: "Comparison is the thief of joy."*

You may not be a mom, but can you relate to those feelings of emptiness, not-good-enough-ness, and unworthiness? Do you know what it feels like to believe you just *lack*?

---

* "Theodore Roosevelt," GoodReads.com, accessed June 15, 2017, www.goodreads.com/author/quotes/44567.Theodore_Roosevelt?page=3

In my emptiness and joylessness, I learned that it wasn't Foster, my son, who needed to take a first step—it was me.

I finally realized that God cared more about my heart and my feelings of emptiness than even I did. I glimpsed that the Creator of my heart, soul, mind, and strength—and of yours—wanted to recapture them all and direct them back to His original intention.

FILL MY CUP, LORD

Years ago, I was sitting in my soul-searching-quiet-time chair, focusing on Jesus, and He showed me something big. (By the way, I highly recommend you find one of these quiet, special places to go to sit with God.)

God graciously reminded me I was designed to love like my Maker loves. The "God kind" of love isn't conditional, wanting something in return. God's love doesn't pour out from a need to have an emptiness filled. God's love overflows out of fullness. It overflows. It is a way to share fullness.

And that kind of love wasn't possible the way I was holding my cup. My love couldn't overflow to others so long as I needed others' love to overflow to me first. A cup can't even *be* filled while it's tilted outward.

That's why the God-kind of love is possible only by holding the cup upward, not outward.

The beauty of being filled by the true Source is that His love is abounding. Imagine Niagara Falls, but bigger. Imagine our cups standing upright, *as they were created to stand*, with God's infinite love gushing into them. Then we'd effortlessly overflow into the lives of others—not from ourselves, but from Him who is the Source, so that He could be their Source too.

God stands ready to fill your cup. Permanently. Fully. With no leaks but lots of overflow. This book will show you how that will happen for you.

WHO AM I TO SPEAK?

So who am I? I'm another person with a cup, trying to figure it out. Just like you.

When I was in elementary school, my mom cried because I had no friends. In truth, I just didn't care about people. But I did care about getting them to fill my cup. I loved being good at things and getting attention for it: skateboarding, drums, basketball, soccer, trumpet, tennis, and computers.

As a white girl, I was a minority in my elementary school. I love that I didn't care about skin color, and I thrived in a diversity I enjoyed. Then I got to middle school and realized that sometimes color sparks conflict. That broke my heart, and it still does.

Looking back, I realize now that I spent most of my young years thinking everything was about me. It wasn't until I went to a Christian camp one summer that I learned I could take the full makeup of me—athletic, outgoing, exuberant, and just plain crazy—and use it all for something other than myself. I had felt unfocused and random, but my brother-in-law Steve redefined me from "crazy" to "passionate," and suddenly everything felt right. I realized I could use my crazy for someone else's glory. Someone, the only One, who deserved it.

In time, I went from camper to staffer at that camp and have now worked there for over a decade, inviting people to tilt their cups in new directions. Away from family, friendships, jobs, and potential opportunities, so they can be filled by the Source, in order to overflow onto a thirsty world.

I got married in December 2010 (on the awesome "countdown" date of 12-11-10), and then in 2015 our son, Foster, was born. Now, in addition to still working at that same Christian camp, I have the opportunity to travel the country speaking to audiences young and old, teaching people how to hold their cups under the flow of God's love.

I've tried a lot, learned a lot, been through a lot, and been a lot of things to a lot of people, and I am only fully content when I see that God is a lot more than anything else I've run after. God is real. God really enjoys time with me. Me. Megan Fate Marshman.

And He feels the same about you.

LAYOUT OF THIS BOOK

I have learned three things about the Christian life that define who I am and how to live in a way that sets my cup upright. Those three things shape this little book.

Your life has a main character. You knew that, right? But I'll bet you didn't realize that the main character isn't you. The story is bigger than you (and me). But that one big story *involves* you, and your part is significant.

I want to be significant. Don't you? I want to live a life that matters. I want a life that is more than merely being aware of myself. Here's my journey and here's my process. Here's how we'll get there:

Part 1: There's only one story and only one main character. The main character isn't you (or me).

Part 2: However, it absolutely involves you (and me).

Part 3: And your (and my) part is significant.

READY TO BE FILLED?

I want to share this stuff with you because of how it changed me. The journey you'll follow in this book shows me going from feeling the need to show my own importance to me discovering the importance of others. I went from being self-focused to being self-less, and that transformation rocked my world.

Did you know that such a thing is possible? It is! And I know you want to be invited into something epically big. If you take these truths to heart, you too will be able to walk into any situation and be fully alive and fully free.

I know you want to be a part of something big. And you want to be a significant part of it, not merely a bystander. So many young people engage in social media (I do too!). And while there's nothing inherently wrong with it, it will never truly satisfy. On social media, you're a bystander to the lives of others. I myself check social media when I'm feeling most isolated. Ironically, I forget each time that doing so makes me feel even more … yep, you've got it … isolated. God calls you—and me—out of a bystander life into the "something big" we hunger for.

The incredible news is that you're invited to play your very own unique part in what God is up to in this world. Did you catch that? You get to be a part of what God is up to! As you tilt your cup upward, the way a cup was designed to sit, God can and will fill it so you can be a part of all He's doing! And I mean He'll fill it to over-flowing, what Jesus promised would be, "a good measure, pressed down, shaken together and running over ... poured into your lap" (Luke 6:38).

We exhaust ourselves running around trying to get other people to fill our cups. It's only when we stop running and seeking love and respect from others, that we're able to fully and honestly receive the gracious love God gives, and can begin spilling over into the lives around us.

Embrace the truths in this book, and you'll overflow with love for your friends, family, parents, kids, coworkers, and enemies—not out of a need to be loved *by them*, but out of the abundance that is the result of being loved *by Him*.

Part 1

One Main Story—One Main Character

IN THE BEGINNING, GOD

The first thing you need to understand if you are to stop tilting your cup outward is that this whole story—life, the universe, and everything—isn't about you or me. It's about what God, the star of the show, is doing.

Like any good novel, the Bible introduces its main character at the beginning. Right at the outset—in the very first words, in fact—we are told whose story this is.

"In the beginning God" (Gen. 1:1).

It does not say, "In the beginning, you …" It does not say, "In the beginning, me …" It's so tempting to believe that we're the main characters of our own stories, isn't it? But how useful is our study of the Bible going to be if we make ourselves the main characters of our quiet times?

I've learned the best way to read God's Word is to search for Him in it. If we search for ourselves, we'll get frustrated and possibly be left disappointed. But if we seek God in it, we'll never be disappointed, because He's all over it and it's all about Him. So let's learn a bit more of what's true about Him.

God is who God was and who God will always be.

Got that? He is constant. His thoughts of you are constant. Other people's thoughts of you are not always constant. How could they be?

But who God is, is always constant. And He has always been so, even before … in the beginning.

GOD CREATED

In the beginning, God … created the heavens and the earth.

What do we know to be true about God? We know God created. And let's see how He created:

> Now the earth was formless and empty, darkness
> was over the surface of the deep, and the Spirit of
> God was hovering over the waters. (Gen. 1:2)

There was darkness, yet God was present. Wherever there is darkness, wherever there is anything or nothing, God is present.

I can say with absolute confidence that even in the midst of your darkness, God is present. He has not left. Don't believe the lie that He's so disgusted with you He's abandoned you. It's not true.

I have more good news:

> And God said, "Let there be light," and there
> was light. God saw that the light was good, and
> he separated the light from the darkness." (Gen.
> 1:3–4)

Notice He created something and then thought what He'd made was good. Not fine, certainly not bad, but good. On the plus side of middle. Maybe even pure good. God makes good things.

> God called the dry ground "land," and the gath-
> ered waters he called "seas." And God saw that it
> was good. (Gen. 1:10)

Hmm. He made it and thought that the thing He'd made was good. Huh.

> Then God said, "Let the land produce vegeta-
> tion: seed-bearing plants and trees on the land
> that bear fruit with seed in it, according to their
> various kinds." And it was so. The land produced
> vegetation: plants bearing seed according to
> their kinds and trees bearing fruit with seed in
> it according to their kinds. And God saw that it
> was good. (Gen. 1:11–12)

Yup, it was good. There He goes again.

> He also made the stars. God set them in the vault of
> the sky to give light on the earth, to govern the day
> and the night, and to separate light from darkness.
> And God saw that it was good. (Gen. 1:16–18)

And …

> God created the great creatures of the sea and every
> living thing with which the water teems and that
> moves about in it, according to their kinds, and
> every winged bird according to its kind. And God
> saw that it was good. (Gen. 1:21)

Are you spotting a trend here? And then finally …

> God made the wild animals according to their
> kinds, the livestock according to their kinds,
> and all the creatures that move along the ground
> according to their kinds. And God saw that it was
> good. (Gen. 1:25)

Wow, those first days, He was on a roll. Everything He created was good! Wish I could have a few days like that, you know? Seems like half of what I create is good, and the other half is just *meh*.

But then God outdid Himself. He made something next that left "good" in the rearview mirror.

GOD CREATED YOU

Did you notice God made animals according to their kind? That means according to their likeness and image and type. They're all of animal-kind. But when He made man, He said it differently:

> Then God said, "Let us make mankind in our image, in our likeness, so that they may rule over the fish in the sea and the birds in the sky, over the livestock and all the wild animals, and over all the creatures that move along the ground." So God created mankind in his own image, in the image of God he created them; male and female he created them. (Gen. 1:26–27)

God made animals according to their kind, but when He designed humans, He made us according to *His* kind. According to His likeness, image, and type.

What do you suppose He thought of that aspect of creation after He'd created it? He'd have to think humans were at least *good*, right? I can't see Him creating something that was poorly made. If that ever happened, and I don't think it would, I'm guessing He'd just poof it away and keep at it until it seemed good.

When God evaluated the humans He'd just made, He said something new:

> God saw all that he had made, and it was very good. (Gen. 1:31)

God created animals good. He created the land good. He created the stars good. Everything's good. Then, when He created people, He called them very good. Here's what I believe "very good" means: whole and complete, lacking nothing.

This means, my dear friend, that when God created you, He said, "Very good! You are whole and complete and lacking nothing you need to honor and glorify God with your life. Just how I wanted you!"

That's not what our culture tells us, is it? Every commercial says, "You need this thing to be good," or "You *could* be good if you had this product," or "Your life would be so much better if you used this service." They promise to make you good or happy or fulfilled, but they also imply that you're *not* good now, or else you wouldn't need what they're selling. If you were already whole, complete, and lacking nothing, why would you need their clothes or their skin cream or their car?

Our entire culture operates on the idea that we all need to do, get, purchase, earn, or achieve some other thing in order to be happy. We talk about the pursuit of happiness, as if happiness is trying to get away from us. When was the last time you saw anything on television or elsewhere in the culture that inspires contentment? Certainly not ads. Movies and novels tell of people who are trying to overcome some challenge to achieve some prize. What was the last movie you saw about a person who didn't want anything more than he already had, so he stayed home thanking God for his abundance? Okay, I admit that would be pretty boring. Storytelling does require a quest. But the point is that when you add together all the entertainment, and especially advertising, it floods us with discontentment.

All day long, we're told we're incomplete and lacking—pretty much the opposite of what God thinks of us. Pretty much the opposite of very good.

Our culture tells us this, and we believe it. So in those few moments when we're not rushing out to buy or achieve the thing that will make us happy or watching commercials that tell us what we need to buy or achieve to make us happy, we're comparing ourselves to each other.

Remember Roosevelt's words, that comparison is the thief of joy. When God made you, He said, "Very good. You lack nothing. You are whole, complete, precisely how I wanted you. Very good." Not just according to humankind, but according to His kind.

GOD CREATED US ON PURPOSE WITH A PURPOSE

When someone makes something, it's for a purpose. A sculptor doesn't start working on a block of marble without a plan. A painter has a subject in mind or standing right in front of his easel. A construction team doesn't just throw girders and uprights together and wonder what's going to happen. Anytime anyone creates anything, it's always created with a purpose.

That includes you! You, dear friend, reading this book, are not an accident. I don't care who told you that you were. Long before you were created by your parents, you were created by the mind of God (Eph. 1:4). He had you and His purposes for you in mind. Maybe you have looked in the mirror and thought, "That's not good enough for me." But remember that God looked at you and said, "Aha, just how I want you!"

God made you with a plan, and that plan is community.

THE ONE THING THAT WAS *NOT* GOOD

After God made all these things that were good and very good, He looked around and saw something that wasn't good at all:

> The LORD God said, "It is not good for the man
> to be alone. I will make a helper suitable for him."
> (Gen. 2:18)

God made humans "very good," but even something very good can be not good if it's not placed in the right surroundings. The human creation was very good, but it wasn't a very good situation when there was only one. When Adam was the only human, he was very good and not good at the same time. Very good in essence, but not good in isolation.

He needed a friend. Some companions. A wife.

Don't get me wrong: God didn't have Adam's marital status in view here. As special as the moment was in the movie *Jerry Maguire*, Renée Zellweger's character did not complete Tom Cruise's character. You are not completed by a spouse. If that were the case, it would be quite odd that the One we follow, Jesus Christ, and the one who wrote a majority of the New Testament, Paul the apostle, were both single.

What God was saying about you and me is that He made humans very good, but very good only when in relationship with other humans.

We're made in God's image, remember? Well, even God isn't alone. I'm not talking about the angels or whatever—I'm talking about the Trinity.

God said, "Let *us* make mankind in *our* image" (Gen. 1:26). Well, who is this "us" and "our" of which He speaks?

You see, God is actually a triune God and always has been. *Triune* means "three in one." There's God the Father, God the Son, and God the Holy Spirit. Before time began, God the Father perfectly loved God the Son, who perfectly loved God the Holy Spirit, who perfectly loved God the Father right back. God the Father perfectly glorified God the Son, who perfectly glorified God the Spirit, who perfectly glorified God the Father.

Why did God create creation? Ever wonder that? I'm not sure we'll ever know until we can ask Him in person, but there's one thing we can know: He *didn't* create everything because He had a need. He wasn't so empty or needy or bored that He decided to create the universe. Hardly!

He had everything, and yet He created us according to His kind.

If God is a community of three in and of Himself, and if He made you in His image, I think that means He made you for community too.

It is not good for you to be alone.

The isolation that defines our society is not good. It's so weird to me that I can be sitting in a room with a thousand other people and still feel completely isolated. Isn't it crazy?

Here's something to ponder: Do you ever think certain thoughts and assume you're the only one who thinks them?

Maybe that's because you don't like to let people really know you.

IF YOU REALLY KNEW ME

If no one knows you well, no one can know how to love you well. We complain about our loneliness, but then we don't let people into our lonely hearts so they could *relieve* our loneliness.

I've worked at Hume Lake Christian Camps in California for over a decade. One particular summer, I started playing, with high schoolers, a game called "If You Really Knew Me, You Would Know ..."

I don't introduce the title of the game at first, of course. Rather, I walk into their cabins and simply ask if they want to play a game.

When that crazy camp person from the stage steps into your cabin and asks if you want to play a game, you expect that game to be bizarre, right?

"Who wants to play a *fun* game?" I say.

And the high schoolers squeal, "Ohmygoodness, I do, I do."

The girls giggle, and I get them to sit in a circle on the floor.

"Here's the game," I say. "It's called 'If You Really Knew Me You Would Know ...' what?"

And there's usually silence after I say that.

"That doesn't sound fun at all," one girl generally admits on behalf of the group.

I act confused yet sassy. "It doesn't? That's okay. Let's play anyway. Don't worry: I'll go first.* Here's how you play. You say, 'If you really knew me, you would know ...,' and then you finish that sentence. If people *really* knew you, what would they know?"

---

* I go first because leaders should never consider themselves the exception. Just because they can doesn't mean they should.

They're looking at each other now. They know they've been ambushed. This sounds way too serious to be considered a game.

"All right," I say, "here's mine: If you really knew me, you would know that I have a dog. Her name is Abercrombie. I named her when I was sixteen—now we're embarrassed, so we call her 'Abby.'"

The girls usually relax then, because they thought I was going to go straight to, "If you really knew me, you'd know my life is a total mess and I oftentimes cry myself to sleep" or whatever. And now they think they're safe again. *Oh, just pets? Surface stuff like that? Okay, fine, I think I can do this.*

So we go around the circle, and everyone talks about their pets. Fun and easy. People start settling into the game.

When the round gets back to me, I say, "Okay, a little deeper this time." I take a big breath. "If you really knew me, you would know that I have a cousin who is mentally disabled, and for that reason, since I was twelve and understood that she was different, I've always hated when people use the word *retarded* to hurt someone."

This sucks all the air out of the room. The girls look at me like, "Okay, are we really going there?"

Let me take a minute to talk about the power of words to harm or to heal. I don't care how powerless you feel or how angry you are; what you say matters. Your words wield incredible power. For good or evil. I wish your negative words weren't as forceful as they are, but that reality is balanced by how powerful your positive words are. Proverbs succinctly says, "The tongue has the power of life and death" (18:21). There are no neutral words.

Really, all of us have no idea how vulnerable people are to what we say and how careful and intentional we need to be with our words.

Back to my game. I say, "I hate when people use the word *retarded* to hurt someone." And as we go around the room, as people talk about that word or other words they'd been hurt by.

Then round three comes, and we go even deeper still. By round four, half the girls are crying.

There are two rules to the game. Number one: share. Be known. Stop hiding. Number two: listen. Because if you listen, you'll learn how to love.

Now, I know that listening is hard, especially if you're completely consumed with yourself. Listening is not just waiting for your turn to talk. Listening is more active than that. Listening is learning how to love. It's seeking things you can learn about other people as they share. It's gathering clues about who they are, how they feel, and what they need. It's asking questions to further understand. It's waiting to respond until they have fully expressed themselves or is ready for you to. When you truly listen, you learn how to love people.

The game is not just about you.

One year I did this at night in a cabin. The next day we were playing field games. A thousand people gathered together, and I was in charge. All the kids were on the field, and I was getting them into twenty-eight teams behind twenty-eight cones to play a relay race.

Suddenly, a kid from team 14 jumped out wearing a banana costume. I thought, *Okay, that's funny. Go ahead.* Instead of trying to rein it in, I just went with it. The banana started running across the field, and of course all the kids were cheering and laughing.

Then from team 23, a kid jumped out dressed as a gorilla. Obviously. So now they were both running. The banana was running for his life from the gorilla. Everybody started chanting, "Banana! Banana!"

The banana tripped and fell. He fell pretty hard and smacked the ground with his face. For a minute, people thought it was part of the gag, so they laughed a little. Someone cried, "Ooh, banana split!" We all laughed.

Then the guy in the gorilla suit shouted to the banana, "You're such a retard!"

I stood there, so angry and sad. And alone. I was still feeling raw about that word, having just talked about it in one of the cabins the night before.

Then a girl jumped out from team 8. She was a sophomore who had been in that cabin the night before. She sprinted from her cone, ran up to me, put her arm around me, and whispered, "You don't have to be alone on that one anymore."

It is not good for us to be alone. If we, God's image-bearers, are content with shallow relationships, we imply that He is a shallow God.

Because when you're alone—when you hide, when you don't share, when you stay out of community—people don't know how to love you. But if you do allow people to really know you, you enter into relationship, and that is very good.

Wake up to the gift of the people right next to you. Not only do you need them to be there for you, to really know you, but they also need you to be there for them. It is not good to be alone, but to change that, you need to be willing to be known.

KNOWING AND BEING KNOWN

God wants us to know each other. He wants us to be in relationship with others, just as He is in relationship with Himself. But God also wants us, His best and "very good" creatures, to be in relationship with Him. We pursue knowing God by being hungry for Him.

I recently had the opportunity to go to Israel. While I was there, I learned from one particular synagogue what religious services would have been like during the time Jesus lived.

Instead of the speaker standing at the front of the synagogue, like how we do church today, he would stand in the middle of the crowd. People would then get in a big circle around the speaker. Maybe this was so they could hear the speaker, since they didn't have sound systems back then.

Think about that for a minute. I don't know, but that image—all these people standing or sitting around to hear from God's Word—always reminds me that *we* are the church. We, the people who go to church, *are* the church. Church is both a building and us.

The synagogue service would start with something we might call praise and worship. But it wasn't always just through music, like we do it. Sometimes it was the community sharing facts about who God is. So someone might stand up and say, "God is real." And everyone would cheer, "Woo." And then someone else would stand up and declare, "God is more powerful than you could ever imagine." And people would call back, "Yes and amen." Someone else would stand up and shout, "God is healer." And that was how one kind of synagogue service would begin: just remembering who

God is. Because … who God was, is who God is; and who God is, is who God will forever be.

After praise and worship, it would be the janitor's turn.

Okay, he wasn't exactly a janitor, though he was in charge of keeping the synagogue clean and holy for services. His other job was much cooler.

His second job was this: he had the privilege of going to the Torah closet, picking up the scrolls that were going to be read that day, and bringing them out to the center to be read. (The Torah is the first five books of the Old Testament.)

Back then, they didn't have Bibles with nice leather bindings. God's Word was on scrolls made of vellum, which is animal skin. So this guy's job was to go into the closet with all the scrolls and bring out the one for that day's synagogue service.

But he would never, ever just walk out with the scrolls. No. He would always *dance* out with the scrolls. Just imagine … the Torah dance! He comes out, and everyone cheers. He starts dancing, and the entire audience goes nuts.

Here's why: the world outside the synagogue's doors was really loud. The reason he would dance, the reason people would cheer, was that they were desperate to hear from and get to know God. In their shouts, they were communicating, "I long to hear from God today!" They were thirsty for God. They wanted to be in community and relationship with the Lord of creation.

Have things changed so much since Bible times? I don't know how you see it, but to me, the world seems louder than ever outside the church doors. Sometimes even inside the church.

I don't have to do more than check social media or watch TV to start hearing the world screaming at me: "You're not good enough." "You're weak." "You have to be perfect or you're worthless." "You're an accident." "You don't have what it takes."

The keeper of the synagogue scrolls would grab God's Word, and he would dance. People shouted and cheered because they were hungry to hear from God. They craved connection with Him.

My friend, it is not good for you to be alone. God made you very good—whole and complete, lacking nothing. You are the only *you* God made. And while this life isn't about you (it's about Him), you do play a major role. God made you to be in relationships—with other people and with Him.

If you've been hearing the world's hateful voice, and if you've been comparing yourself to others and feeling like you don't measure up, then you've been tilting your cup outward for other people to fill. It won't work, and you'll just feel more and more terrible. You have to live in agreement with how God made you, which is to be really known (be in true community) and to really know your Creator. So what went wrong?

WE MADE IT ABOUT US

It all started way back in the garden of Eden. The sinister voice of a slithering serpent whispered to us back then that we could be in control—that we *should* be in control. It told us we could be equal with God. We listened to that voice then, and we've been listening to it ever since.

That's why it's so incredibly important that we read God's Word.

The number-one question high school students ask me is this: "How do you hear from God?"

My answer? Start with the Bible. It is God's Word to you. And in a world that's screaming lies at you, it's vital that you don't pull an Adam and Eve and believe those lies.

Let me ask you: What lies have you been believing?

Maybe if you told someone those lies, you could begin to leave them behind. Maybe just hearing them with your ears and seeing how false they are will help you push them away. And maybe letting someone in on the secret could help you be known so that you can be loved better by someone around you.

I once sat in a restaurant with a friend who had become overwhelmed with lies in her head. In a moment of deep trust, I asked, "What do you think about yourself?"

"I'm worthless," she said. "I'm unworthy of love, I'm boring, and I simply don't matter."

Hearing this surprised me, as she was someone who energetically loved other people incredibly well. So many people would be quick to argue with her own assessment of herself, and I got the feeling that a lot of people had tried to in the past.

"Let me ask you something." I pointed to the waitress. "Would you ever say that to her?"

"Say what?"

"Would you look at that waitress, someone you don't know at all personally, and tell her she is worthless, unworthy of love, boring, and simply doesn't matter?"

"Of course not."

"Why not? Couldn't she be those things?"

"Absolutely not. God created her. She matters. She is someone with limitless potential."

I took her hands in mine. "Then why do you say and believe those things about yourself?"

FOUR RESPONSES TO SIN

When God confronted them for listening to the serpent and eating the forbidden fruit, Adam and Eve went through four different responses.

Shame on Me

First, they were ashamed of their sin. (By the way, I define *sin* as any thought, word, deed, or attitude that goes against God's perfect standard.)

> Now the serpent was more crafty than any of the wild animals the LORD God had made. He said to the woman, "Did God really say, 'You must not eat from any tree in the garden'?"
>
> The woman said to the serpent, "We may eat fruit from the trees in the garden, but God did say, 'You must not eat fruit from the tree that is in the middle of the garden, and you must not touch it, or you will die.'"
>
> "You will not certainly die," the serpent said to the woman. "For God knows that when you eat

from it your eyes will be opened, and you will be like God, knowing good and evil."

When the woman saw that the fruit of the tree was good for food and pleasing to the eye, and also desirable for gaining wisdom, she took some and ate it. She also gave some to her husband, who was with her, and he ate it. Then the eyes of both of them were opened, and they realized they were naked; so they sewed fig leaves together and made coverings for themselves.

Then the man and his wife heard the sound of the LORD God as he was walking in the garden in the cool of the day, and they hid from the LORD God among the trees of the garden. But the LORD God called to the man, "Where are you?"

He answered, "I heard you in the garden, and I was afraid because I was naked; so I hid."

And he said, "Who told you that you were naked?" (Gen. 3:1–11)

Did you see that? "Who told you that you were naked?" Who embarrassed you? Who shamed you? Why are you hiding? Why did you make these ridiculous leaf-pants?

Wow, *shame*. Talk about a powerful word. As soon as you read it, I know there's a chance a very vivid picture popped into your head. Maybe *shame* loads a whole lot of baggage into your mind. We've all felt shame, that terrible, soul-hating sorrow for something we've done. We've all also been *shamed*, made to feel like a subhuman unworthy of life on earth over something we've done or not done, or just over something we are.

Those are the worst: being shamed for something we can't help. Like our gender or race or size or level of beauty or athleticism or grace or intelligence. For our financial situation or our parents or where we live or our accent or our skin complexion.

Shame may be the single worst weapon that can ever be used against another person. Yes, worse than an actual weapon. A gun can shoot you only once or a few times, and then that's all it can do. But shame hits you hard and goes deep … and keeps shooting you over and over, sometimes for the rest of your life.

If we believe the lies of shame, the lies people have said about us because they're just as broken as we are and suffering from the shame others have put on them, we will forever be tilting our cups outward. Why? Because if shame came from someone else, then we expect someone else to be able to take away the shame. Or at least to give us some relief from it. If a person can paste the shame on me, then maybe other people can peel it off and throw it away.

But guess what? No other person can take away shame. Only Jesus can do that. And even He didn't do it simply by saying something nice about you and me. He took away shame by *taking the shame* Himself. He took it on Himself. And when He died, so did all the shame that ever has been or ever will be delivered to any of His children. Oh, people still dish it out, and sometimes it lands on us. But Jesus already killed it, so just shrug it off in the direction of Jesus's cross. Because shame doesn't belong to you anymore. He takes it all, and He kills it.

Adam and Eve felt shame for their sin. That's why they hid. We still do that today. When we feel shameful, we hide. We try to look perfect. We do extra holy stuff. We try to impress people and get people to like us and say nice things about us, because when that happens, we feel just a little less shameful, at least in that moment. But it comes back because it never left. It doesn't leave until we toss it onto Jesus, who shreds it on the cross.

Don't Blame Me

Adam and Eve's second reaction to being caught in their sin was to blame others. Let's pick up the story again in Genesis:

> "Who told you that you were naked? Have you eaten from the tree that I commanded you not to eat from?"
>
> The man said, "The woman you put here with me—she gave me some fruit from the tree, and I ate it."
>
> Then the LORD God said to the woman, "What is this you have done?"
>
> The woman said, "The serpent deceived me, and I ate." (3:11–13)

They blamed each other. "It wasn't my fault," Adam said. "It was that woman's fault. And really, since You gave me this woman, God, I might have to say You share some of the blame too."

Then Eve chimed in: "Uh! Don't blame *me*. It wasn't my fault. The Devil made me do it!"

And on it goes. It's a good thing they didn't have a dog, because they would've kicked it. That blame game went all the way down the list to Satan (whose name means *accuser*), who probably just sat there snickering while proudly living up to his name.

What about you? Do you ever blame others for your own wrong choices? "I wasn't going to do it, but my friends made me." Or "I didn't want to be the only one who didn't try it." Or "He said he was going to move on to some other girl if I didn't."

Or the even more serious kind of response, where you feel others in your life have done so much wrong to you, so much injustice, that you're just broken. If you're broken, what's the point of trying to do right? That was crushed out of you long ago, right? Really, society has failed you. Your family should've protected you. Your friends betrayed you. You were dealt a bad hand. So, really, there's no reason for you *not* to act in these ways and take back a little of what has been cheated from you, right?

Yeah, blaming others. It's a powerful way of justifying bad choices.

It's also something people do when they feel shame and guilt. When you feel so awful about yourself, all you want to do is make that feeling go away. If you can put some or all of it on somebody else, it makes you feel better, if only for that minute.

And here's a surprise: the only way to be permanently rid of shame actually *is* to let someone else take the fall for it.

Someone already did, in a little place called Calvary.

Jesus on the cross is Jesus taking the blame. He was the dog everybody kicked. I don't mean that in a comical way or a sad way.

He volunteered to be the one who everyone could throw their shame and blame onto. Adam and Eve didn't know yet God would do that for them. But now you and I can know it. Go ahead, blame Him. Let Jesus take the shame. His shoulders are broad enough.

Hide Me, Please

The third reaction Adam and Eve had to sin is one I've already mentioned, but I want to look more closely at it now: they hid. They threw on some leafy underwear and dove into the bushes.

Silly, right? Not something you and I would do, right? So when someone says, "How are you?" and you respond, "Good," you're not hiding. Nope. "I'm fine; how are you?" Totally not hiding.

Don't hide. You have to play "If You Really Knew Me, You Would Know …" for people to be able to know you and love you well.

But if you do hide, don't complain that no one knows you or loves you well.

The Fear in Me

The fourth reaction Adam and Eve had to being confronted with their sin was that they were afraid. They had fear.

They did what they knew they shouldn't, and then they heard the Lord walking in the garden. Yikes! Into the bushes they jumped, knees knocking. What would He do to them? Better to avoid Him altogether. When He called them out of the hedge, their fear and shame caused them to try to deflect the fault onto someone else. Then when He started handing out punishments—pain in childbirth, frustration in growing crops, enmity and anger and expulsion from the garden—the fear flared up even more.

Do you have fear? My dear reader, do you or someone you know understand the word *fear* really intimately?

The solution to this kind of fear—the anxiety that comes from standing naked before the all-knowing God—is the same as the solution to feeling shame, wanting to blame, and wanting to hide. You know His name.

Here's the best part of the Adam and Eve story: it didn't start with sin (it started with God creating us "very good"), and it definitely doesn't end with it.

It ends with hope.

Yes, they listened to lies. Yes, Eve grabbed the fruit. Yes, she handed the fruit to Adam. Yes, he ate the fruit. And we've been copying them ever since. But even in the midst of all that punishment, God provided for them (He made real clothes for them), and He promised to redeem them in the future (He promised to crush the serpent).

Those things He has also done for you. At the cross, Jesus crushed the Devil, defeated death, took all shame and blame upon Himself, satisfied the punishment for sin, and gave you Himself as a covering and white cloak as you continue to walk the earth this side of Eden.

Jesus is the end of shame, blame, hiding, and fear, and He is the author of your hope.

Part 2

God's Story Definitely Involves You

Not long ago, I was sitting in a hammock in my backyard in California watching my husband roll the trash can from our backyard to our front yard.

It was a very tranquil moment. I was loving that my husband actually takes out the trash. But as he was moving the trash from the back to the front, something happened that caught my attention.

When my husband was halfway there, Foster, our son, who was one and a half years old at the time, ran up in his fleece monster onesie because he wanted to help. *Aw, how cute.*

Up to that point, my husband had been moving rather quickly. It had been one of those go-getter days, when you don't even stop to think because you're just being so productive. Rather than seeing our son as a nuisance, which would have maintained my tranquil moment, he slowed down and invited our little man to play a part in taking out the trash.

My husband tilted the trash can to the point where our son could put his little hands on the grungy handle and "help."

They moved slowly. So, so slowly. At first, sitting in the hammock watching all this, I thought it was cute. But then I recognized how incredibly inefficient it became.

Something more than just taking out the trash was happening.

Then I saw my husband's eyes as he looked down at his son. He didn't care that it took longer. In fact, he seemed overjoyed to be having that special moment alone with his son, side-by-side, hand-by-hand. They smiled and continued. Ever. So. Slowly.

The next day, I was scheduled to speak at a college chapel service. Just before I stepped onstage, I asked the Lord for a word: "Lord, what do You have? What do You want to teach me before I go teach others? What do You want to share with me so I can share it with others?"

I listened earnestly. *"You get to take out the trash."*

"Yes! A metaphor.… So good. Boom!" I thought of the sin-drenched audience and looked forward to taking out their trash!

But just as quickly, it was as if the Lord said, *"Um, no,* you're *playing the part of your son in the illustration."*

I was confused. "What do You mean? Are You saying I make You less efficient?"

That was when I realized the truth in what I'd seen the day before: God is the only one who can actually take out the trash. I couldn't take out the spiritual trash or the emotional trash or the trash of the past or the trash of the present. I couldn't. My husband couldn't. No more than my son could take out the physical trash on his own. So how did I think I could stand on a stage and take out the trash for an auditorium full of college students? How could I think that I could, sitting in a coffee shop with my friend, take out the trash that needed to get out of her life?

Sometimes I get to be part of taking out the trash. *If* God invites me in. *If* I do it in partnership with Him. God, the one who is fully capable of doing it all by Himself, chooses the less efficient route … us. Why? Because that's how He works. God cares more about our personal, intimate relationship *with* Him than our productivity *for* Him.

On that chapel day, God invited me to participate in what He was up to.

Sometimes I convince myself that I can take out the trash, that I'm really helping, with my own abilities. I'm sure Foster, my little son, thought he was really helping too. But if his dad were to have let go, the whole thing would have simply dropped to the ground.

God is standing right beside us, hand in hand, inviting us to play a part in the most epic story ever told.

There is one ginormous story happening all around us. It's not our story. No one person on earth is even the main character. Not you, not me. But the God of the universe invites us to play a part.

We get to help take out the trash because relationship with you and me is so important to Him. He loves to do a partnership, a duet, with you, as He's spinning out His epic tale. He not only invites you to play a part in His story; He also pursues you to be in it.

GOD PURSUES IMPERFECT PEOPLE

Let's go back to the garden:

> The LORD God called to the man, "Where are you?"
> (Gen. 3:9)

That's what I'd like to ask you, my wonderful reader: Where are you? In this insane world of sin and shame and brokenness, where are you? What lies have you been believing? Where have you been running to find approval? Where are you as you hold your cup? In a place where you hold outward or upward?

Because the weird part about holding the cup outward is that other people's approval actually does satisfy. It actually does make you feel okay about yourself if you can get enough of it from the right people at the right time. It will make you feel just good enough to get by, maybe, but only for a minute. But sometimes it's only satisfying enough to keep you coming back for more. It's exhausting.

But here's something I've learned about this one big story we find ourselves in: yes, God's the main character, but the good news is that God pursues imperfect people. And who God was, is who God is; and who God is, is who God will forever be. So, no matter where you are, no matter where you've been running to in your search for assurance that you're a good-enough person, the fact is that there is a God who comes toward you. Who pursues you. When everyone else might want to run away from your mess, God draws near you.

The Bible is not a story of people seeking God. This is the story of a perfect God who pursues imperfect people.

That includes you. And me.

So I ask you again: Where are you? God has placed you in a place, in a body, in a family, in a nation, in a situation—in this one time in history—and He has invited you to join Him in a story about reaching out to a world that needs hope.

THE ENTIRE STORY OF THE BIBLE INVOLVES YOU

Several years ago, when I was engaged and planning my wedding, I decided I wanted a very unconventional bridesmaid. I wanted Nanny, my grandmother, to stand with me as I got married.

Now, at that time, Nanny was ninety-four. She was from England, spoke with a thick English accent, drank Diet Sprite, and ate cinnamon-sugar toast in her house, which was right next door to my parents' house.

One day, I went over to ask her about it. *Knock-knock-knock.* An hour later (or so it seemed) she opened the door.

I acted all surprised and said, "You made it!"

And she said what she always said to me: "You're ridiculous."

"Nanny," I said, "do you want to go to breakfast?"

She nodded. "All right. Let me get my coat."

Another hour later (not really), she had her coat and her purse and her walker, and we were finally outside her house heading to my car.

She braced herself on her walker and raised an eyebrow at me. "Race you to the car."

I shook my head. "Oh, Nanny, I'm so sorry. I don't know if you realize this, but I put my fast shoes on today. They are very fast. Are you sure you want to race me?"

"Indeed."

So we started walking, and I was kind of letting her get ahead. And then, ever so slowly, she started cutting me off with her walker. She eased into my path and then really started trying to put the pedal to the metal.

She was pretty fast, I have to admit.

I still beat her, though. I told you: fast shoes.

We finally got to breakfast, and I asked her to be in my wedding. She was delighted and agreed to being the first ninety-four-year-old bridesmaid she had ever heard of.

But the story takes a sad detour. I asked her in August to be in my wedding, but in September she had a stroke.

You know those days when nothing else seems to matter except the one burden on your heart? Have you had those days? The day I found out about her stroke was one of them for me. Nanny, who was supposed to walk down the aisle in my wedding, was in a hospital bed, alive only because of a bunch of tubes.

I remember just losing it in the hospital. My sister held me up as we hugged. And I was angry. "Why?" Have you ever asked that question of God?

And I recall my dad said, "Hey, we're not going to know anything for a while. So why don't we all go do what we normally do, and we'll meet up tonight?"

At the time, I was teaching at a Christian university. I think I cried during the entire forty-five-minute drive to the campus.

When I got to my classroom, I sat at my desk, holding back the tears, and my students walked in like it was just another day. It wasn't their fault. For them, it probably was a normal day. They couldn't know what was happening in my life. But I looked down at my notes and then up at my students, and for some reason, I couldn't go on like normal. *This doesn't matter,* I thought. *None of this matters with Nanny in the hospital. I'm just going to leave.*

But by then, the students were all there and it was time for class.

I stood up with my notes like I was going to teach, but then I dropped the notes on the floor and said, "Forget that!"

A really nervous girl in the front row looked at me, very worried. "Do we write that down?"

"No, don't write that down." I sighed. "I'm dealing with bad news, and I need good news. We're at a Christian college, so we should all know about the good news called the gospel. So will someone share the gospel with me? I'm in need of some good news."

They all looked at each other.

"Anyone?" I asked.

Nobody would meet my eyes. This whole room full of college students slowly put their heads down on the tables.

"Come on. I need the gospel. I need really good news that somehow meets really bad news … and wins. Someone give me the gospel. Somebody remind me why Jesus came. Why He died. What His resurrection has to do with me today. Why it changes me. I need it to change me today."

Still nothing. So I started calling on people.

"Ryan?"

Ryan's eyes got really big.

"Yes, Ryan. Stand up and tell us the gospel."

He sank into his chair. "Nah, I'm good."

So I turned to Aimee, then Haley, then Braxton, then Josiah. Nobody was willing to attempt to share the gospel.

If I asked you to tell me the gospel, what would you say? If you claim to believe something, shouldn't you be able to explain it? I don't mean that you know every last theological argument and have the whole Bible memorized. I just mean, do you know the essence of this faith you say is the answer for all humankind?

When I was young, I heard a Christian speaker share the gospel. He did it in a captivating and clear way, and he gave us specific Bible verses that explained the essential truths. I wrote those references down on a page in the back of my Bible. (They were all from Romans: 1:19–21, 25; 3:23; 5:8; 6:23; 8:1; 10:9–11; and 12:1–2.) After that, if I was ever asked who Jesus was or why He matters or why I'm living for Him, I would go back to that page in my Bible and utilize those Scriptures.

That sad day in class, I opened my Bible and read each of those seven passages to my class. If they couldn't give me the good news, I was going to give it to myself straight from the Word of God. At that point, I was worried about Nanny and sad for my students (who weren't sure how to share the gospel explicitly) and also disappointed with myself (for not having taught it to them). So I read those verses, gathered my stuff, and just left them all sitting there.

Throughout the rest of that class hour and into my break period, I received texts and e-mails from them. They said things like this:

- "I've been a Christian my whole life, and I have no
  idea how to articulate the gospel. Never done it."

- "I gave my life to Jesus a long time ago, but I have this sin issue that I feel like I'm a slave to, and it's not getting fixed. I know I'm forgiven for it, but where do I go and how does the gospel change me in the midst of my struggle?"
- "I've never given my life to Jesus. I have agreed that He came to earth for me, but I have no idea what it looks like to 'surrender my life.' Sounds scary, and honestly, I'm pretty content just living the way I've been living."
- "I've been a Christian my whole life and, to be honest with you, I don't know, Megan, where to even start in my Bible. Because I've been a Christian so long, people expect me to know by now how to read my Bible, but I don't know how. Where do I start? I feel too old and too far along in my faith journey to admit that I don't know how to spend time with God."

I read each e-mail and text and got more and more convinced of what I needed to do. So you can imagine what my poor second class encountered in their teacher. I had become … Super Preacher.

As they walked into the room, I was thinking, *Oh, you get ready, suckas, because you have no idea what's about to happen.*

They sat. I threw my notes and preached: "Do you know the gospel?" I spoke with all my heart and simply let God share His good news through me. People's lives were changed. Praise be to God!

But not because of what I said. I can't change lives—not yours or anyone else's. No preacher or teacher or anyone else can change your life in the God direction. Oh, people can tell you truths like, "God loves you," but no one can convince you. That's God's job.

As my experience that day in class demonstrated, the big story of God is something He's doing, but it still involves you, and the Bible tells all about it.

GOD'S BIG STORY

This guy named Paul is a great person to teach us what God's big story is about.

Now, Paul had baggage. Before he became a Christian and had his whole life altered, he was called Saul, and he hated, *hated* Christians. He considered them a terrible threat to the Jewish religion and way of life. Then Saul met Jesus in a dramatic way and was radically changed, and he went on to write the majority of what we now call the New Testament.

You know what that tells me, my friend? It tells me that God can do whatever He wants with whomever He wants, whenever He wants.

Do you know someone who seems so far away from God that it appears as if he or she can never come to Him? Don't stop praying for that person. Ever.

Paul wrote a bunch of letters to different churches that were around in the decades after the death, resurrection, and ascension of Jesus. Most of these letters, believe it or not, still exist (well, copies of copies of copies of them). One of these letters was written to the church in the very pagan city of Rome and is now known as the book of Romans.

In the early chapters of Romans, Paul shared a huge, sweeping summary of biblical history. Those words provide an essential key to God's Word: don't think of the Bible as this random collection of stories. It's actually one big story with one main character. Each supporting actor and each smaller episode make much of God and carry the bigger plot forward.

Here's a bit from early in Romans:

> What may be known about God is plain to [all people], because God has made it plain to them. For since the creation of the world God's invisible qualities—his eternal power and divine nature—have been clearly seen, being understood from what has been made, so that people are without excuse. (Rom. 1:19–20)

In other words, creation screams, "Creator!"

If you just look around yourself, you'll see everything that is made had to have a maker. My iPhone screams that it was created. It didn't just appear from nothing—someone made it. My car, my computer, the highway, the skyscraper … someone made them.

In the same way, our lives scream that someone made us.

Remember, when God created you, it wasn't because He had a need. God created you and me and all people because He wanted to share what He already had—love. He created you *in His image* so you

could live not out of a need to be loved by people but to share the love
He gives.

So, Paul told us in Romans, people just know that they were made
by a Creator. But what happened? Something went wrong.

> They exchanged the truth about God for a lie, and
> worshiped and served created things rather than the
> Creator. (Rom. 1:25)

The truth about God is that He's enough. The truth about God is
that He's all you need. The truth about God is that He is in control.
Are you okay with those truths? Is that what you believe? Or are you
exchanging those truths for lies? That He's not enough, that you need
more than He gives, or that He's not really in control, not of your life.

Have you believed that you're in control? That your life and present choices and future opportunities are all up to you?

Those Paul wrote of (just like us today) exchanged the truth about
God for a lie and served created things rather than the Creator. Bad
move.

And we've all made the same bad move at times in our lives. It
wasn't just Adam and Eve who sinned, and everyone who came after
them has been perfect. Ha! Paul said that:

> All have sinned and fall short of the glory of God.
> (Rom. 3:23)

Wait, all of us? Even Grandma? Even the preacher at the pul-
pit on Sunday mornings? Even the Christian singer on the radio?

Even great saints of the past? What about Mother Teresa? Surely *she* never sinned. What about Paul himself, who wrote this letter?

Yeah, sorry: *all* means *all*.

Everyone except Jesus who has walked, is walking, or will walk this earth has sinned or will sin.

If we could be sinless, we wouldn't need a savior to take care of our little sin problem. But if *all* have sinned, then all of us need a savior.

In order to be in a relationship with a pure and holy God, guess what—you have to be perfect. There's a perfect standard. But we all fall short. Everyone on this planet ... we all have one thing in common: we all fall short of the glory of God, and we all need a Savior.

When I was in high school, I played the comparison game. I'd look at someone and think, *At least my sin's not* that *bad*. I saw my sin as tiny compared to others. So guess how big I thought I needed Jesus to be in my life? Exactly.

We all fall short. We all sin. We all need a Savior.

That's why Jesus did what He did:

> But God demonstrates his own love for us in this:
> While we were still sinners, Christ died for us.
> (Rom. 5:8)

I love that it doesn't say, "But God *said* He loved us a lot." No, God *demonstrated* His love. Talk is cheap. So many people say they love but don't act like they love. "God demonstrates His own love for us in this: While we were still sinners, Christ died for us."

Why did Jesus have to die? I mean, it was such a brutal death, and everyone hates to see the innocent suffer.

Jesus had to die because if He didn't, the "falling short" that all of us have done would've resulted in us being forever separated from God, even after death.

> The wages of sin is death, but the gift of God is eternal life in Christ Jesus our Lord. (Rom. 6:23)

The result of—the payback for—our sin is death. That's what our falling short earns us. One day, we will all die physically. But this refers also to spiritual death. What we earn from living our lives with sin is eternal separation from God.

But …

Do you see that word in the verse above? Yes, we've earned damnation forever … *but …* the story doesn't end there. *But* God doesn't leave us there in that condition. He created us, and we turned away, earning punishment, *but* He doesn't even force us to pay that ultimate debt. He pays it Himself.

Where we should've gotten hellfire, He gives a gift.

Is that what you do? When someone makes you really angry, do you just go out and buy them a thoughtful little gift you know they'll like? I don't.

Why did Jesus have to die? Because He was the gift. His death was *our* death, which He took in our place. Our punishment, our payback for falling short, got put on Him, and then *He* was killed in our stead. But it didn't end with His death: He defeated death and rose from the grave and lives forever at God's side. Now, because

He did that, you and I can receive the gift and stay eternally in His presence.

Really grasp that truth: what we'd earned was forever death, but what He gave us instead was forever life.

In order to be in a perfect relationship with a perfect God, you have to be perfect. We all fall short. And because the only one who lives up to God's perfect standard *is* God, God sent Himself. Jesus—who alone was fully God and fully man—came to this earth, and He alone lived a perfect life, thereby earning a perfect relationship with the Father. We earned separation, but He didn't give us what we'd earned.

And then He rose from the grave, proving two things: number one, He is God, and number two, He has the power to make dead things live.

STAIRWAY TO HEAVEN

In every religion, there is a ladder to God or some kind of paradise. A stairway to heaven. Every faith system on the planet—including Christianity—has instructions and steps for how you can obtain the ultimate pinnacle, be it eternal life, release from the cycle of rebirth, or whatever else. All of them teach you how to take steps toward that goal.

In all cases but one, the emphasis is on what the person does to climb that staircase. Follow the Five Pillars of Islam or the Noble Eightfold Path of Buddhism or the Ten Commandments of Judaism or escape from the Samsara cycle of Hinduism, and you will obtain your goal. Maybe.

The difference between all other world religions and Christianity is that in Christianity, the person doesn't climb up the staircase to be saved for eternity and reach God. In Christianity, God climbs *down* the stairway to take people back up with Him.

The gods of all other religions sit at the top of a mountain, so to speak, waiting to see if anyone can be good enough to scale the cliffs and mount the summit. The God of Christianity left the mountaintop, came all the way down to the lowest depths of earth to get us, put us all on His back—any who would take His offer—and brought us up to the summit Himself.

There's still a ladder. But because God knew that you and I could never climb up to His perfect standard—because we all have sinned and fallen short—Jesus climbed down the ladder to be with us. Because you and I couldn't get there on our own merits and efforts.

I can't get to perfection. Jesus came to earth and lived a perfect life, the only thing that allows for a perfect relationship with God. That means, humanly speaking, He had earned heaven. He's the only one in the history of the world who actually did that. But He didn't come here to take His earnings and run. He'd already *had* heaven before coming here. No, He came with a mission, and the first part of that mission was to live a life that earned heaven.

Jesus takes that which He deserved, eternal life, and offers an invitation for you to exchange it for what you deserve, which is God's wrath.

Sometimes, even in Christianity, we lose sight of this simple, perfect swap. Sometimes we think Jesus's sacrifice and substitution for us is great and all, but it's only a start, and if we really want to get to heaven, we'll do more stuff on top of it. If you'll only read your Bible enough. If you'll only go to church enough. If you'll only become a missionary. And then, oops, you really blew it that one day—so now you're knocked down a few rungs on the ladder. Just buckle down and try harder and maybe one day you'll get God to let you into heaven.

Bah! That's turning Christianity into Buddhism! Or into some other world religion that isn't Christianity. Christianity isn't about how many times you've been to church or how good you are or how many Bible verses you've memorized. Christianity is about a free gift offered to you by a God who climbed down the ladder to take you up to where you could never get on your own.

That's the big story of God, and now you see how He is the main character.

But if you're like most Christians in America, you've heard a slightly different message. You've been taught or led to understand that simple faith in Jesus's great exchange is fine and all, but what really counts is going to Bible college or leading people to pray the prayer of salvation or having a daily quiet time.

It's crazy, people adding stuff to Christianity to make it seem harder than it is. That silliness is what led C. S. Lewis to write this passage in his book *The Screwtape Letters*, in which a greater demon gives a lesser demon instructions on how to mess up a Christian's life:

> What we want, if men become Christians at all, is to keep them in the state of mind I call "Christianity And." You know—Christianity and the Crisis, Christianity and the New Psychology,

Christianity and the New Order, Christianity and
Faith Healing, Christianity and Psychical Research,
Christianity and Vegetarianism, Christianity and
Spelling Reform.*

Christianity and spelling reform—I love it.

Right, that's how many of us are led to believe we have to climb
the ol' stairway to heaven. We have to add church attendance to our
salvation, and *then* we'll be considered Christian. The problem is
that once we begin allowing people to tell us there's something else
beyond our simple faith that we have to do to be saved, we have no
way of saying no. If Person A's additional thing (say, faith plus church
attendance) is right and binding on us, then who's to say that Person
B's thing (faith plus Bible memorization, for example) isn't binding
too? Then Persons C through ZZZ come along adding their hoops
to jump through, and pretty soon Christianity has become nothing
but constant hoop-jumping.

Know what I mean?

You've tried it, haven't you? *I need to pray more. I need to read my
Bible more. I need to confess more. I need to give more. I need to volunteer more.* If only you do this, and if you do it perfectly, and then if
you do this other thing, and then one more thing, all perfectly, then
maybe you can get to God and be used by Him. The problem is that
the ladder to God is infinite.

Aren't you tired of it?

Ditch the climbing and take the free gift instead.

---

* C. S. Lewis, The Screwtape Letters (Uhrichsville, IL: Barbour and Company,
1990), 126.

> There is now no condemnation for those who are in
> Christ Jesus. (Rom. 8:1)

If you put your faith and trust in Jesus, you can know this: when God the Father looks down on you, He doesn't see you, with all your inability to live sinlessly—He sees Christ. The Christian is *in* Christ Jesus, and God lavishes all His love and treasure on Jesus and anyone in Him. When He looks at us now, He says, "Blameless! Holy! Cleansed!"

I don't know about you, but when I look at my own past, I wouldn't use those words. But when God the Father looks at you and you step into a life of following Christ, suddenly, there is no condemnation.

You can be forgiven. Yes, even you. It doesn't matter what you've done. There's nothing you have done or could do that would make Him love you any less. His love bucket for you is filled to the top and sloshing out, and there's a hose running into it, keeping it overflowing. And there's nothing you can do about it.

There's no more love to gain. There's no leak in the bucket that makes you have to keep topping it off by doing good deeds. There is no condemnation. Think about that.

What's the only correct response to such generosity? To fall down and accept it with great gratitude.

The only rung we have to worry about to attain salvation from Christ is the bottom one. We simply step *down* off it and say, "Yes, Lord; thank You. I'll receive what You're offering."

> If you declare with your mouth, "Jesus is Lord," and
> believe in your heart that God raised him from the

dead, you will be saved. For it is with your heart that you believe and are justified, and it is with your mouth that you profess your faith and are saved. As Scripture says, "Anyone who believes in him will never be put to shame." (Rom. 10:9–11)

I love that last line: *"Anyone who believes [trusts] in him will never be put to shame."*

That, my friend, is the good news I needed that day when Nanny lay in the hospital.

By the way, Nanny did, in fact, walk down the aisle at my wedding. She recovered enough to be in the ceremony, which was in December. She had to have two guys escort her down. When she drew close to me in the aisle, she winked … boasting that I had only one man that day but she had two.

RUNNING THE HILL

That's the gospel, then: simple faith in the God who climbed down the ladder because you and I couldn't climb up it. Not Christianity *and* anything—just faith alone.

I wanted the high schoolers I worked with at that Christian camp to truly understand this. So we tried something crazy.

We would gather all the female students outside in front of a large fire in the evening. We'd flick on these big floodlights, and we'd say, "What if we told you that all these things—sin, shame, guilt, fear, anxiety, and every other sin—could be gone? Would you girls be interested in that?"

The high schoolers were always highly skeptical. What's a camp counselor going to do to take away some of the worst plagues of their lives?

We'd designate one of the counselors to represent God. That God character would say, "There are two rules in this activity. Number one: be all in. Don't hide. Bring everything before me. How can I clean out anything you don't bring before me? And number two: you don't have to listen to anyone else but me."

Then the God character would leave, and we'd hand out white T-shirts and black Sharpie pens. The campers would put the shirts on and partner up. Then we'd announce the next part of the activity.

"In order for us to get rid of sin," we'd say, "we need to know what it is. Remember, sin is any thought, word, deed, or attitude that goes against God's perfect standard. Turn to your partner and take turns confessing your sins to each other. As you confess your sin, your partner is going to write it on your white T-shirt, and then you'll flip-flop. Okay, you guys do that, and we'll be back in a minute." Then the counselors and I would leave.

So we'd hide in the bushes and just watch. First, the girls would look around with they-can't-be-serious grins. Finally, a few girls would begin. The girls always started with "safe sins." It's odd how we justify sin and assign levels and degrees to it. They'd start with something like, "I lied once." The other person would write "LIAR" on the shirt. (It's always easier to talk about other people's sins, isn't it?) After a few safe ones, they'd run out of ideas, so they'd look at the other shirts around them, and they'd say, "Ooh, I did that one too," and they'd write it.

After a couple of minutes, we'd step forward again. "Stop hiding, girls! Rule number one: be all in. Stop going halfway. If you always do what you've always done, you'll always get what you've always had. Let's do it; be brave."

This time, we'd leave them for ten minutes. This time when we came back, I could tell from their posture and tone, even without reading their shirts, that they had stopped hiding. We shut off the floodlights and asked, "How do you feel, now that no one can read your shirt?"

"Better!"

We'd turn the lights back on. "How do you feel now?"

"Terrible. Ashamed."

"I understand. But remember, we told you we would make this all go away. So raise your hand if you have baggage. Maybe it's emotional baggage. Maybe it's guilt baggage. Maybe it's sexual baggage. Anyone?"

Hands would go up all around the group. We'd send volunteers out into the crowd and give a backpack filled with rocks to everyone with a hand up.

We'd continue. "All right, who looks in the mirror and thinks, 'That's not good enough'? You know that God says you are valuable, but you and the mirror disagree with Him. Anyone?"

Hands would go up. So we'd hand out mirrors that were shattered.

"All right," we'd say, "who's a slave to people-pleasing? At the expense of pleasing God, you'd rather please people?"

Hands went up, and we'd literally tie their hands with chains.

Can you picture an outdoor clearing filled with high school students chained up, holding broken mirrors, and schlepping rock-filled backpacks?

"It is so draining, isn't it?" I'd say.

"Yeah!"

"Do you want to get rid of it all?"

"Yeah!"

"Do you *really* want to get rid of it?"

And they'd shout, *"Yeah!"*

I'd point at this epic dirt hill we were gathered at the base of. "If you want to get rid of all that weight you're carrying … run up that hill!"

They'd groan but start up the hill. The other counselors and I would line the trail and cheer them on, and up they'd go.

At this point, the God character would reappear. I wouldn't say anything about that character, and he wouldn't speak either. But it was amazing to me that nobody remembered rule number two.

There they were, losing in a big game of Simon Says—because God hadn't told them to carry the rocks or accept the mirror or the chains, and God certainly hadn't told them they could work those things off by this giant effort. They listened to someone else, breaking rule two, and very quickly they started paying the price.

As they all ran by, first up and then down, then back up again, the other counselors and I (but not the God character) would yell things at them to keep them going.

"Run harder! Save yourself! You can fix your sin if you just try harder. Run up that hill; run up that big stairway to heaven—you're going to get there. I know it's infinitely long, but you can do it! Run harder! Don't stop!"

At first, all those high school girls ran with determination. "I *can* do it."

And we'd yell, "Just beat that girl! Run faster than her. Make sure you're more impressive than her. Make sure you have more followers. It's not about the team—it's about being the best one on it. Yes, be a friend and help someone, but don't let her beat you!"

Before long, they'd have dirt on their faces and in the creases of their eyes. Every time they'd get to the top, we'd yell at them to run back down, and every time they'd get to the bottom, we'd yell at them to start back up.

And all the time, the God character would just watch them run.

I'd yell, "Hey, stop slacking. This time, run like you care."

"We thought we were," they'd say, "but okay."

"Run back! What are you doing? Run harder! Move faster! Do more! Read your Bible more! Care more! Be more impressive. You can fix your sin! Just be a little bit better."

How long do you think they would do it? Two minutes? Ten minutes? Most of them would go at least fifteen minutes, and all the while we were shouting, "Come on, just try harder. Just try harder. Just try harder. Just be better. You can make your way to Jesus."

It's silly, isn't it? Why would anyone agree to do something like that when they didn't have to? And did the mirrors or chains or backpacks full of rocks go away just by them running up and down that hill? Of course not. What made them think that working harder would cause their load to feel *less* heavy?

Yet that's how I used to be with God. That's how so, so many young people—and adults—are today. They've listened to some other voice that has told them they can climb their way to God if they just do these hard things.

That's not Christianity, my friend. That's Budd-Jude-Hind-Slam or something, but it's not Christianity.

Where can you run to fix yourself? What hill can you climb that is high enough to pay for your sins? What pack is heavy enough to take away your guilt?

Do you dislike thinking about this? I've found that some people go to great lengths to avoid looking too closely at what they're doing in life. They distract themselves with friends and activities and relationships and school and work and whatever else. Because they'd rather be distracted than depressed. They'd rather be apathetic than fail.

Don't be afraid to focus on this. If you're lugging around a backpack of rocks and carrying chains and broken mirrors, wouldn't you rather get rid of them and be free? Because that big hill is a metaphor for life. So many people are running up and down trying to beat everyone yet ironically going nowhere and accomplishing nothing that lasts.

At our camp, we did this activity for ten weeks and with hundreds of students. One moment with one young girl stood out, probably because watching her was like lifting a mirror to myself. This young girl ran really fast. She beat everybody up and down the hill, and I could tell she took pride in her ability. As she ran by the God character, He stopped her right in the middle of the trail.

"Why are you running?" he asked.

"I can do this!" she said, and I saw she believed it. Maybe she just meant she could beat everyone and win whatever prize we might be offering to the winner, or maybe she was thinking metaphorically too, like she believed her own efforts could win her some relief from her burdens and from the sins written on her white T-shirt.

"God" let the girl go back to running. Everyone continued hurrying right past him. I always found that interesting, and probably very symbolic. Am I running past God too? Am I so busy doing stuff for Him that I ignore *Him*?

So the God character stood there, being passed by these young people huffing and puffing, and he'd whisper, "Why are you running?" Most people wouldn't be listening, so they'd trudge by without even knowing he'd said something. Ouch, right? Are we listening? Do we even expect that God might say something to us?

Once, this one fast girl came by, and the God character whispered, "Why are you running, and where is it getting you?"

She paused. "Well, they told us to run."

"Who did? Me?"

"No, not you. The other ones. The ones in charge."

The God character nodded. "Where is it getting you?"

"Up and down, up and down," she said. "I'm really tired."

"I'm sure you are. Do you know why I sent My Son, Jesus?"

"Sure," she said, spouting something off from memory. "You sent Your Son to die on the cross for my sins."

"Which sins?"

She smiled. "The sins of the world!"

He leaned in close. "Which sins, my girl?"

Then it was as if a light went on in this girl's mind. Suddenly, she got it. She'd believed all the right things her whole life, but it had never made it from her head to her life. She had made Christianity about nothing but what she did for God, not what God has done for her.

The essence of your faith is not how hard you try. That's any religion except Christianity. The essence of Christianity is that, because you couldn't achieve, Jesus achieved on your behalf. And your goal, your part, your response is to put your faith and trust in His cross, in His sacrifice, and in His resurrection.

Yes, that's right: you can stop running to achieve what Jesus has already accomplished.

Right there on the dirt trail, as sweaty people jostled past her, she slid that backpack off and dropped her rocks. She took the chains off and let them fall to the ground. She set that broken mirror at the feet of "God."

And then, with a look of relief and purpose, she turned to those around her. "Everyone," she yelled, "stop running!"

She got it.

But we had to keep playing our part as distractions and false voices, so we shushed her. "Quiet, girl!"

That made her yell all the more. "The world—those people—they lied to you!"

"Shh, you're giving it away."

"They're liars! You can't fix yourself! Stop running!" She started grabbing people's chains and trying to pull them off.

But the girls running by resisted her. They held tight to their chains. Why? Because they were more comfortable with their chains. Because it was what they were used to.

"You don't have to carry them!" It was amazing, watching her. She was this tiny little thing, but she was on fire. "You don't have to! Jesus carried the chains and demolished their locks. You can stop running! You can't fix yourself. The world lied when it said it's all about being the best and getting to the top, being more impressive, having more followers, more likes. The world lied to you."

She quit trying to pull their chains away and instead just started grabbing whole people and dragging them to "God." She no longer tried to fix them herself—she didn't have that ability. But she could bring them to the one who could.

That's the life of a Christian. It's not about what you can do for Christ but about what He's already done for you. It's not about hauling your own sin around and trying to work it off; it's about walking in freedom in response because it's already off and then bringing other people to Jesus who still haven't heard (or believed) this really good news. Jesus made it all possible for you to be a part of what He is up to in the world. Responding to what Jesus has accomplished is your part.

Why are you running? Where is it getting you? Do you know why He sent His Son? Are you carrying things around that God never asked you to carry? Are you bearing the marks of your sin though Jesus has already wiped them away? Step into your part of the story as you let go and let God play His.

YOU'D BE SURPRISED WHO DOESN'T KNOW THIS YET

As I mentioned, Nanny recovered from her stroke and was able to walk down the aisle at my wedding. As I entered married life, I decided I wanted to start hanging out with Nanny on Tuesdays.

We had a delightful time together every Tuesday, enjoying Diet Sprite and cinnamon-sugar toast and jokes about which sport she had been playing that broke her nails *this time* and otherwise cutting up.

But one Tuesday, four months after the wedding, I came into her room and found her crying. "Nanny, what's wrong?"

"Oh, Megan," she said, "I thought I was living for your wedding. I thought I'd been allowed to recover so I might participate in your lovely ceremony, and then I would go. But it's been months now, my dear, and here I remain. Why am I still alive?"

"Nanny, I—"

"Think about my life, Megan. I am confined to a wheelchair. I sit in this chair all day, and I wait for people to love me."

An image came into my mind of my dear, blessed Nanny sitting there in that chair with her cup held outward for others to fill. It had never occurred to me that she might not have learned the thing I was just coming to understand for myself.

"Nanny," I said, feeling as nervous as I can ever remember feeling, "do you know God?"

She sniffed. "Yeah."

"Okay," I said, "do you know why He sent Jesus?"

And she said, "Now that one confuses me, because He's God, but then He was a man, and I'm not really sure why He went ahead and died if He's God."

There it was: my opportunity. I shot a prayer upward, ran to my car, grabbed my Bible with those verses written in red in the back, hurried back, and plunged ahead. "Nanny, can I tell you a story?"

She blew her nose and nodded.

"There's a God, Nanny. A perfect God who loves you perfectly. He wants to have a perfect relationship with you, but there's a problem: we all fall short because of this thing called sin. Do you know what sin is?"

"Do you mean the fact that I'm really selfish?"

I smiled. "That's right, Nanny."

"I always feel guilty for that."

"Me too, Nanny. But that's where God butts into the story. He sent His Son, Jesus, who lived the perfect life you couldn't live and died the death you deserved and rose from the dead, proving He's more powerful than sin, its effects, and even death itself. If you put your faith and trust in Jesus's sacrifice, instead of your own abilities to try to be good enough for heaven, you can be saved. For if you confess with your mouth that Jesus is Lord and believe in your heart that God raised Him from the dead, Nanny, you will be saved." I looked at my grandmother. "Nanny, do you believe this?"

"Yes," she said with tears streaming down her face. "What do I do?"

My nervousness flared up again. I stand in front of large audiences and give this presentation often, and yet in front of Nanny, my heart was going nuts. "We can pray," I finally managed to say.

"Wait!" she said.

But I didn't want to wait. God's timing was right then. "What is it, Nanny?"

She looked worried. "I don't know what to say."

"Just be honest."

She closed her eyes and said the most beautiful prayer I'd ever heard: "God, I'm really selfish. And now I know that's why You sent Your Son, who died, and because of that, God, help me not to wait to be loved but to love others first, because I know I'm already loved. Help me. Amen."

Five years later, Nanny passed away. Just ten days shy of her one-hundredth birthday. We all wanted her to live to be one hundred because we thought that would be cool. But she always said, "I don't want to be one hundred—because that's old."

I miss her, believe me. But I have confidence that she's with Jesus, waiting for me. Probably trying to serve Him Diet Sprite and cinnamon-sugar toast. I don't know if that really was the first time she'd ever made a faith decision or if she'd made one at a young age and had just forgotten her part of the story. But what an opportunity I had with Nanny.

That same opportunity is before you right now.

> If you declare with your mouth, "Jesus is Lord," and believe in your heart that God raised him from the dead, you will be saved. For it is with your heart that you believe and are justified, and it is with your mouth that you profess your faith and are saved. As Scripture says, "Anyone who believes in him will never be put to shame." (Rom. 10:9–11)

Have you ever put your faith and trust in Jesus and His sacrifice? Or did you give your life to Jesus awhile ago but have gotten caught up running again? Have you been living as lord of your life and now you're tired? Maybe you have been running aimlessly up and down that hill (called life) and you're exhausted, and you thought maybe you could get there, maybe you could fix yourself, maybe you could find a way to climb the endless ladder to a better relationship with God on your own. And if you couldn't get there, maybe you've felt okay if you could just get a little higher than the people around you.

Run to Jesus, my friend, and talk honestly with Him about where you've been and where you are, just like Nanny did. Whether you want to surrender your life for the first time or pause from running in order to encounter Jesus again, don't wait a second longer. Talk to Him. Then I'd recommend having a conversation with someone you trust about how to further respond to Jesus's invitation.

Imagine putting this book down and loving others not because they deserve it but because you finally realize you never did and never could. That's grace. That's love. That's the greatest story ever written, and it's still being written … through us.

But perhaps you're like my students that day in class, and you've known Jesus all your life, but you don't really understand how to live out that love in response. Maybe, up to now, you've missed a big portion of your part in God's story because you've been distracted in the midst of running. God invites you to encounter Him! Today, right now, you're invited to play your part by continually encountering Him so that grace and love and mercy can overflow from you into the lives of other people you see running. Your part of God's story, living in response to what Jesus has done, is ready to be lived.

> Therefore, I urge you, brothers and sisters, in view
> of God's mercy, to offer your bodies as a living sac-
> rifice, holy and pleasing to God—this is your true
> and proper worship. Do not conform to the pattern
> of this world, but be transformed by the renewing
> of your mind. Then you will be able to test and
> approve what God's will is—his good, pleasing and
> perfect will. (Rom. 12:1–2)

This is our part: offering ourselves to Him, walking in freedom and hope and joy ourselves, grabbing people around us who haven't learned the secret yet, and bringing them to Jesus. You may still exert some energy—you may even run—but you'll do so with purpose and in love and in the knowledge that you're not running to work off your guilt or sin or debt, but you're running to bring the good news of freedom to others in response to Jesus's defeat of your guilt and sin and debt.

Still, you are not the main character of this universal story—God is. But the story definitely involves you. That's why Jesus came: to invite you to be a part of what He is doing and how He is redeeming the world. If you want to be part of God's story, you have to first come to Him in faith. And once you're found in Him, others will find Him in you.

Part 3

Your Part Is Significant

An old theater saying states, "There are no small parts; only small actors." This is, I think, designed to bandage the wounded pride of an actor who tried out for the lead role but was cast in a supporting role instead. "Very well," this adage is supposed to help her say, "then I'm going to be the very best 'Woman Number 3' this town has ever seen!"

Now, I'm not sure that little proverb has actually helped anyone feel better, but it does make a point: you don't have to be the star of the show to know that your part is important and to do the best you can.

When it comes to the Christian life, as we've seen, we are not the stars. God is. He's spinning out this incredible tale, and He's invited us to be in the show with Him. But, perhaps unlike Woman Number 3, the part He's asked you to play is deeply significant.

The great thing about coming to understand that God feels you are important is you can stop trying to *prove* your importance to everyone you meet or who might possibly see you online. Right? Right.

ANYTHING THAT HAPPENS WITH YOU

One way God makes your role significant is by using things that happen to you to help in the lives of others.

Whatever it is you go through is not only about you, and what it brings to your life isn't meant to stop with you. It's always meant to go through you and into the life of another. Those things include your past, your gifts, your family, your struggles, your health, and anything that happens in church the next time you go.

When the events of our lives—including our bad decisions—are brought to God for His use, amazing things happen.

Take, for example, the biblical story we call "The Woman at the Well." The story comes from John 4 and starts like this:

> Now Jesus learned that the Pharisees had heard that he was gaining and baptizing more disciples than John—although in fact it was not Jesus who baptized, but his disciples. So he left Judea and went back once more to Galilee. Now he had to go through Samaria. (John 4:1–4)

Quick geography lesson: the northern part of Israel was called Galilee. This was where Jesus grew up and did most of His ministry. The southern part of Israel was called Judea. That's where Jerusalem was, and still is, along with Jericho, Bethlehem, and lots of other places you've probably heard of.

But in the middle of Israel was this portion of land called Samaria. Samaria used to be part of Israel. In fact, the capital of Israel used to *be* Samaria before King David made Jerusalem the capital.

Over the centuries, civil war split the kingdom that had been united under David and Solomon and then, at one point, another empire swooped in and conquered Samaria. The conquering kingdom brought in their pagan religion, and many beliefs got mixed together in Samaria. Centuries later, the whole place was conquered by the Roman Empire, who couldn't really tell the difference between Jews and Samaritans.

However, the Jews and Samaritans definitely could tell the difference, and both groups believed the other group had left the true faith of God and Moses and the Scriptures. Because Israel was larger than Samaria and had more people and more power, their version of events got to sort of win.

But the two groups hated each other. If a Jew needed to travel from Galilee to Judea, he could easily do so in just a couple of days … if he went in a straight line … which meant trekking through Samaria.

Ha! Not going to happen. Jews would rather tack days and miles onto their journey than set foot in that tainted land of blasphemers!

So it must've really confused the disciples when Jesus "had" to go through Samaria, as we saw in the Scripture quoted above. *No, He doesn't* have *to go through Samaria,* they probably thought. *What we* have *to do is avoid Samaria altogether.*

Does the disciples' attitude speak to you at all? Do you have people you'd rather avoid than talk to? Would you rather add an hour to your trip than come anywhere close to that person? And then have you ever had someone drag you right past that person's nose?

Yet John says Jesus had to go through Samaria. Huh. Whenever you read that Jesus, King and Creator of the universe, *had* to do something, it's a good idea to take notice. Because Jesus didn't *have* to do anything. But apparently He had to go through Samaria. Why?

> So he came to a town in Samaria called Sychar,
> near the plot of ground Jacob had given to his son
> Joseph. Jacob's well was there, and Jesus, tired as
> he was from the journey, sat down by the well. It
> was about noon. When a Samaritan woman came
> to draw water.... (John 4:5–7)

He was tired. I love that we can relate to Jesus, and He can relate to us. He was tired so He sat down. It was the Jewish sixth hour, which would've been noon. While He was sitting there by a water well, a woman from the town came up with a bucket.

This is a clue to our story, but it's easy to miss. Typically, a Samaritan woman of that time would go to the well first thing in the morning before the blazing heat of the Middle East got going to draw water to provide for her family. But this woman came to the well at noon. Why?

Because she was hiding—a lot like Adam and Eve tried to hide from God. She was going well out of her way to hide from people, while Jesus was going out of the normal Jewish way to meet her. She figured no one else would be there at that time because it was hot and it was noon.

> Jesus said to her, "Will you give me a drink?" (His disciples had gone into the town to buy food.)
>
> The Samaritan woman said to him, "You are a Jew and I am a Samaritan woman. How can you ask me for a drink?" (For Jews do not associate with Samaritans.)
>
> Jesus answered her, "If you knew the gift of God and who it is that asks you for a drink, you would have asked him and he would have given you living water."
>
> "Sir," the woman said, "you have nothing to draw with and the well is deep. Where can you get this living water? Are you greater than our father Jacob, who gave us the well and drank from it himself, as did also his sons and his livestock?"
>
> Jesus answered, "Everyone who drinks this water will be thirsty again, but whoever drinks the water I give them will never thirst. Indeed, the water I give them will become in them a spring of water welling up to eternal life."
>
> The woman said to him, "Sir, give me this water so that I won't get thirsty and have to keep coming here to draw water." (John 4:7–15)

I love the sort of playfulness going on here.

"You want water? How about living water?"

"Living water? You don't even have a bucket for regular water. But sure, I'll take your magic water, crazy man. It'll save me a lot of time!"

> He told her, "Go, call your husband and come back."
>
> "I have no husband," she replied.
>
> Jesus said to her, "You are right when you say you have no husband. The fact is, you have had five husbands, and the man you now have is not your husband. What you have just said is quite true."
>
> "Sir," the woman said, "I can see that you are a prophet." (John 4:16–19)

Hoo, it's getting juicy now, isn't it?

Did He really go there about her sordid past? Oh, yes, He did.

Jesus knows all about you … and He still pursues you, even when you're not pursuing Him. That's interesting to me. He knows you completely and still loves you … completely.

I'll bet this woman was thinking, *Uh-oh, this guy's some kind of mind reader. I'd better change the subject fast!* So she pulled out her surefire distraction, the oldest argument between Jews and Samaritans:

> "Our ancestors worshiped on this mountain, but you Jews claim that the place where we must worship is in Jerusalem."

"Woman," Jesus replied, "believe me, a time is coming when you will worship the Father neither on this mountain nor in Jerusalem. You Samaritans worship what you do not know; we worship what we do know, for salvation is from the Jews. Yet a time is coming and has now come when the true worshipers will worship the Father in the Spirit and in truth, for they are the kind of worshipers the Father seeks. God is spirit, and his worshipers must worship in the Spirit and in truth."

The woman said, "I know that Messiah" (called Christ) "is coming. When he comes, he will explain everything to us."

Then Jesus declared, "I, the one speaking to you—I am he." (John 4:20–26)

Jesus solves the Jew-Samaritan question and then moves on to more important matters.

I can only assume that this woman, after being called out and her argument heavily debated, is ready for the conversation to end: "Well, that's your opinion. I guess we won't really know until the Messiah comes, huh?"

Then, Jesus, with the ultimate mic drop, responds: "I ... speaking to you ... am He."

I am He. "You wanted to ask the Messiah? Well, here I am: ask me."

I love it.

Why did Jesus have to go through Samaria? So He could have this conversation.

Yes, He was on the way to Jerusalem, where major events were going to go down. But He didn't wait until He reached His destination to start living out His purpose. Jesus lived His purpose *on the way* to where He was going.

How do you want to have lived your life? When you get to your last day and someone asks you how you lived, what will you say? Will you say, "Oh, now that I'm here at the end, I want to start serving God"? Will you say, "Oh, yeah, every time I arrived at an important destination on the journey, I pulled out the whole living-for-God thing and put on a show?"

No, that's not how it works. How you will have lived your life, when you get to that last day, is measured by how you lived today. Not at those epic moments only, but in every moment along the way. I've heard it said that how you do anything is how you do everything. Therefore, how you live today matters. You want to have lived a life serving God? Then how are you serving Him today? How are you serving Him when no one is watching and no one will notice that thing you did today?

Jesus was on the way to somewhere else, but He stopped and took advantage of the opportunity that walked right up to Him. When it comes to the needs of people, no one is a distraction. Jesus lived His purpose on the way—not as soon as He arrived, met the right people, got the right job, had a kid, or was offered a significant opportunity.

ARE YOU INTERRUPTIBLE?

I was once on a flight to go speak at a conference full of pastors. I was very excited about the chance to fly out to this important conference and stand on that important stage and talk to those important people. I have to say, I felt pretty important myself. All I had to do was get there … and polish up my speaking notes on my laptop.

So I found my seat on the plane, took out my earbuds, and put them in, communicating to the person to my left and to my right that I was busy, okay? I fired up my presentation in PowerPoint and typed this question for that important speaking engagement coming in the near future: "Have you missed out on ministering to families in the midst of doing family ministry?"

I was very proud of that one. I was thinking, *This is so good. This is really gonna get 'em.* Because who of us in ministry hasn't gotten so focused on the tasks that we overlook the people around us? So I was really going to skewer those pastors—I mean, I was going to challenge them, and all their home churches would benefit as a result. *Ahem.*

As I was admiring the question I'd typed, the guy next to me leaned over. "Excuse me."

I thought, *Great, I'm sitting by a person who doesn't get social cues.* So I pulled one earbud out and held it barely away from my ear, as if I was going to just pop it right back in. "Yes?"

"Are you, like, a Christian?"

I almost laughed. I was doing really important work, so I had to get rid of him quick—plus maybe communicate one more time that I was not to be bothered. "Sure am. Praise the Lord. God is good. Okay, back to my work." And I popped that earbud back in.

Hey, I was on my way to minister. I was going to nail those pastors for missing out on ministering to families in the midst of doing family ministry. Ha!

The guy tapped my shoulder. "I have a daughter."

I mean, seriously, could the guy not take a hint?

"She's a Christian too." Apparently, he *couldn't* take a hint. "She actually serves in the children's ministry at her church."

"Wow. That's neat." *Please leave me alone.*

But he kept talking about his daughter. She's the best. She's in the top 3 percent of her high school class. She's an incredible athlete. Blah, blah, blah.

That was when the bricks fell on my head. I don't remember what snotty comment I was thinking of saying out loud, but I do remember I read—and finally *saw*—the question I'd written on the screen.

What a self-consumed punk I'd been. It's embarrassing to admit.

I shut the computer, took both earbuds completely out, and looked at the man.

I had heard as he shared (but hadn't wanted to deal with it) that all he did was compliment the things his daughter was good at. I'd worked in youth ministry long enough to know if a dad only complimented his daughter at what she was good at, then that was where she would run for her confidence: being the best.

Which works just great when she is the best, like when she's a big fish in a little pond. But when she leaves high school for college, maybe she's not the best anymore. Or maybe she is, but only just barely. What happens to her confidence when swimming among one hundred "big fish" from small ponds, each one just as good as or better than her?

As I listened to this man, I thought, *Oh, his daughter! His poor daughter.*

That's when I realized I still wasn't getting it. First, I'd been stuck on my own future ministry and wasn't willing to be interrupted by this person droning on. Then I'd been stuck on how I thought this person was unintentionally damaging his daughter. Finally, the Lord convicted me. He said, "Just see *him.*"

The word *encourage* means "to give courage." If you give people courage only to be the best, guess where they will run to for courage? Being the best. We must be careful with our powerful words. A phrase I've begun to implement when I encourage a friend is, "Here is how I see Christ in you …" Not only does it give courage to us to look more like Him, but we'll also inevitably run after Him to find courage in response.

Are you interruptible? I sure wasn't. I was focused on my destination and wasn't living out my purpose on the way there.

After ten minutes of me just seeing him and responding to him with compassion, this collected and polished man, who turned out to be a lawyer, was bawling. He poured out his heart to me about his brokenness over his children and his marriage and his fears and his worries about being away so much, and that opened the opportunity for me to speak words of truth to him.

Because I was—finally and almost against my will—interruptible.

Are you interruptible? Do you "have" to go through Samaria? Are you open to the God moments He wants to sit you next to? Or are you going to serve Him only when you get to someplace "important"?

BACK TO SAMARIA

Jesus loved to ask questions. He asked 307 of them, as recorded in the Gospels. He wasn't so fond of answering them though—not directly anyway. People asked Him 183 questions, but He gave a straight answer only 3 times.

So our Master of Questions fires one off to the Samaritan woman at the well: "Will you give me a drink?" (John 4:7).

What a simple, basic, incredibly *loaded* question. Will you, a Samaritan woman hiding from the townspeople and jumping from bad relationship to bad relationship, give Me, a male Jewish rabbi, a drink? Will you let Me see your face, or will you hide in shame? Will you set aside your racial hatred, which Samaritans have for Jews, and vice versa usually, and do a kindness for Me after all our centuries of hate? Will you, an unmarried woman, be so brazen as to speak directly to a Jewish man with no witnesses or chaperones around? Will you, who worships wrongly, stoop to serve Me, who you know feels you worship wrongly? Will you, townsperson, do your duty to host a traveler and stranger, though He might disapprove of you?

Yeah, really simple question.

Jesus was interruptible, but this question also asked whether or not the *woman* was interruptible.

Not long ago—after I should've learned my lesson on that plane—I was sitting at my local coffee shop working on some speaking notes on my laptop, earbuds in place. I had been thinking about the Samaritan woman, and I'd just written this statement: "Simple questions oftentimes lead to divine encounters, if we're looking for them."

Very impressive, no? I was pleased.

Then a lady walked up. (Of course someone did, right?) "Excuse me, do you know how to use a Macintosh?"

Not a Mac. Not a MacBook or iPad. A Macintosh. Who calls it that, anyway? (You can tell my attitude right away, can't you?)

I pulled out one earbud, just a half inch, and smarted off. "Yep, sure do." I popped my earbud back in and leaned over my laptop as if I was doing the most important thing in the history of time.

Out of the corner of my eye, I saw her go back to her table. Yes!

That was when the Holy Spirit convicted me. Instantly, I felt terrible for how I'd treated her and even for how I'd thought about her.

You guessed it: at that moment, I read what I'd written on the screen. Divine encounters are there if we're looking for them. *Gah!*

Why did God always interrupt me to do ministry when I was trying to plan out some ministry?

Oh.

Now, let me pause to point out something. What I felt here was conviction not shame. I was deeply sorry I had done this, but I didn't feel shameful and worthless. The Holy Spirit convicts; He doesn't shame. If you are experiencing shame, it's not from Him. He convicts in order to create awareness in us that leads to love and health and, ultimately, a deeper relationship with Him. The Enemy shames in order to create a sense of unease, inadequacy, and unworthiness at the heart of your being. When we listen to shame, we feel the need to prove our worth. Conviction is liberating not crushing. It is a way to break the chains of lies that have been put on us. In God's kingdom, failure is an event, never a person.

I took out my earbuds, dropped them like a microphone, and walked to the woman's table. "Ma'am, I actually do know how to use a Mac ... intosh. How can I help you?"

"Oh, great," she said. "I got this new computer to help me write this paper comparing Islam with Christianity. I'm just trying to find the truth, you see."

Of course you are! Yikes. So I sat down to help her (with her computer and her questions), and we had an amazing discussion.

But look how close I came to missing this opportunity! So long as I kept my life revolving around me, who knows how many chances like this I'd miss?

On the road from your prayer chair to your "ministry" lies a host of chances for God to interrupt you with glory like this. If you're interruptible. Divine encounters are all around, if you're open to them. You could miss them. You *will* miss God's plans if your life revolves around your plans. There's one thing, one *Being*, our lives should revolve around.

Sometimes these incredible encounters begin with very simple questions.

"Will you give me a drink?"

PEELING BACK THE LAYERS

The Samaritan woman responded to Jesus's question with a deflection, by raising a debate:

> "You are a Jew and I am a Samaritan woman. How
> can you ask me for a drink?" (For Jews do not asso-
> ciate with Samaritans.) (John 4:9)

Some people turn to debate rather than open themselves up. Have you noticed? "You and I shouldn't be talking because you look different from me," the woman at the well said. "We're from different cultures and faith systems." She wasn't willing to be vulnerable with this stranger.

But Jesus not only asked questions; He listened to the answers. Because when you listen, you create an opportunity to love people.

Likewise, when you are willing to speak to others and reveal your secrets and your hurts—to be known—you allow others the opportunity to love you in return. Not in the sense of getting your cup filled by others, but in the sense of being known and loved, which is a taste of how Jesus knows and loves you. As I said earlier, it matters for you to share your life. If people don't know you, they won't know how to love you.

Often, I don't give people the opportunity to love me because I don't let people know me. The minute I pull back the layers and people understand who I really am, I'm vulnerable. And I don't like that feeling.

The Samaritan woman didn't like it either. But Jesus continued the conversation.

"Will you give me a drink?"

"Well, we're at a well and you have no bucket, so where's your cup? Where can you get this so-called living water?" she questioned.

"If you knew who it is asking you for a drink, you would've asked Him, and I would have given you living water." Not temporary water. Abundant, living, everlasting water.

"Uh, great. Remind me again: where's your cup?"

I imagine Him just smiling. "I want to create in you a spring of water welling up to eternal life. Not just for you, but for everyone here. And not just for now, but forever."

Then she says, "Sure. I'll take a little bit of what You're offering."

Ever done that? Ever just dip your toe in the deeper things of God? Ever just try it out instead of plunging in?

Sometimes, honestly, that's where I stop at church. Jesus has something for me? Great, let me write it down. Let me sprinkle-sprinkle. Let me take a tiny sip. And then I'm going to go back to just trying harder: "Thank You, Jesus, for just the little bit. But I'm good now."

I have learned that God doesn't want to be just part of your life or mine. He wants to be the whole thing. He's not interested in you sprinkling a little bit of Jesus truth and maybe making your life a little bit better, like a pack of gum you decide to buy as you stand at the cash register. No, no. Because when Jesus says, "Come, follow Me," He doesn't say, "Just sprinkle a little bit on and see if you like it." When He asks you to follow Him, He says, "Carry a cross" (see Luke 14:27). And I can't picture a comfortable way to carry a cross. Yet sometimes that's what we want.

So Jesus gets all up in your business, just like He got all up in the woman's at the well:

> He told her, "Go, call your husband and come back."
>
> "I have no husband," she replied.
>
> Jesus said to her, "You are right when you say you have no husband. The fact is, you have had five husbands, and the man you now have is not your

husband. What you have just said is quite true."
(John 4:16–18)

This woman had been running to temporarily satisfying wells. She thought each of those men would satisfy her and would keep her life-bucket filled, but apparently none of them did. Maybe when the conversation with Jesus started, she'd half wondered if she could hook up with this Jewish traveler—maybe this one would be the right one who would bring her the lasting satisfaction she'd been holding her cup outward to others to receive.*

Where have you been running? If I really knew you, what would I know? What things have you found that satisfy for a moment but then run dry or turn against you?

If only they wouldn't satisfy at all, we'd have no confusion! I mean, if our cups never felt full when we, say, won awards and got standing ovations, then we'd never be tempted to constantly chase awards and standing ovations.

Sadly, it's actually possible to keep enough of these temporary things going that we almost always feel *some* level of elevated cup-filling, even for a pretty long run. Think of famous athletes with unbroken strings of championships. Think of movie stars who are the current "it" stars. Think of rich people becoming more and more successful and rich. Still, some of them actually feel terrible about themselves.

---

* Jesus was the seventh guy in her life. The number seven in the Bible is significant because it represents completeness and perfection.

Of course, some of them may not be nice people. They may have left destroyed families and marriages in their wake. They may be insufferable, self-aggrandizing jerks. Not all of them, for sure, but we've all heard of some of them. Yet somehow even they manage to keep at least a low level of juice coming in that carries them until they can score the next big hit.

But if we really *knew* them—the rich, famous, and beautiful ones I'm talking about—we'd know how miserable some of them are. We'd see them in their suicidal lows. We'd see their system just doesn't work, not really. And definitely not in the long run.

A cup tilted outward to receive filling from others works only long enough to keep you coming back for more. Plus, it's not enough and it's not permanent. It keeps spilling out. Even if it were possible to receive enough at all times to keep it filled, which it isn't, it would leak away. Only the maker of the cup knows how to use it and keep it filled.

You may know you're forgiven, but are you walking in freedom? You might know you're loved, but are you walking confidently and abundantly in it? I bring this up not to shame you but to invite you into something new, something better.

To be honest, I've heard the story of the Samaritan woman at the well a lot. For a long time, I just didn't relate to her. I thought she had deep issues and I didn't. Know what I mean? In my mind, my sin was really small, and so that's how little I felt I needed Jesus.

For far too long I thought I couldn't relate to this woman. Until I sat with the Lord, this passage, and my thoughts about this woman and received a profound thought. I realized that she, like me, deeply longed for love, acceptance, and significance. Have you been there? Moments later I realized these longings are not bad. They're only problematic when I look for them to be satisfied from anyone other than Jesus. As it turns out, it's okay to be needy as long as you know where to be filled.

Do you need Him? Really? How much? Just a little? Are you needy right now? Are you thirsty for more of Him? Jesus said those who hunger and thirst are blessed because they will be filled.

When this woman stood before Jesus, He didn't stop at shallow truths. He dug deep. I like that about Him, because it means I don't have to hide anymore. When you encounter that kind of grace, you overflow with it.

> Then, leaving her water jar, the woman went back
> to the town and said to the people, "Come, see a
> man who told me everything I ever did. Could this
> be the Messiah?" (John 4:28–29)

We all have water jars. We've been calling them cups. As we've discovered, when used wrong, they can't ever get filled. We need to stop trying to get filled with a cup held outward, and all efforts to do so need to be abandoned.

So the woman sets her jar aside and goes into town. That's big. Because remember, she's been hiding from these people. She went to a well at noon to avoid them. But now something has changed, and she's willing to brave the humiliation and the gossip and those sideways looks and talk to them directly. When we really meet Jesus, we're changed.

She hurries into town and starts the conversation by mentioning the very thing she had been ashamed of: "He told me everything I ever did." Now that she's been transformed, she looks a lot like Jesus, who also died to Himself, was buried, and rose to new life, despite His scars. And in a way, now so has she.

Your past will be either Satan's greatest weapon against you or God's most powerful tool for His glory. It all depends on how you're holding your cup. Because anything, and I mean anything, that has happened to you is not meant to stop with you but is always meant to flow out of you and into the lives of others.

The woman at the well was now like Jesus in another way: she started with a question. "*Could this be the Messiah?* Could this be the Christ? Our theology is different from the Jews' theology, but all of us are waiting for the Messiah to come and sort everything out and lead us to the truth. Guys, I think I may have found him!"

> They came out of the town and made their way toward him…. Many of the Samaritans from that town believed in him because of the woman's testimony, "He told me everything I ever did." So when the Samaritans came to him, they urged him to stay with them, and he stayed two days. And because of his words many more became believers.
>
> They said to the woman, "We no longer believe just because of what you said; now we have heard for ourselves, and we know that this man really is the Savior of the world." (John 4:30, 39–42)

Remember the girl on the hill who grabbed the other runners, told them they could stop running, and brought them to the God character? That's what this woman did. Sometimes it's our job to bring our neighbors to Jesus not to fix our neighbors. In fact, God doesn't call you to fix them. God calls you to love them and then entrust the fixing to Him. Your part is significant. Your part is bringing them to Jesus—and it often starts when you show them you need Jesus too.

ON THE WAY TO SOMETHING IMPORTANT

Are you interruptible? Are you looking for the divine encounters all around you? Are you all about His purposes?

In the story of the Samaritan woman, Jesus models for us what it looks like to live out our purpose on the way to where we're going. He *had* to go through Samaria. Maybe He knew that woman would be there, and that's why He went, or maybe this was a random encounter, and because He was looking for a God moment, He found one, and many from that town came to salvation.

Our job is to serve Christ, making much of Him as we go and using whatever is necessary to get people to living water.

People don't need to be impressed with you. What good news is it for them if they're impressed with you? And you don't need to impress *them,* because no lasting worth can come from that. People don't need to think you're awesome; they need to know what they would know if they really knew you. They need to know you're needy.

That sounds strange, I know. But I relate to needy. I don't relate to gathered or perfectly put together. I relate to messy. I relate to a woman who has been hiding because of all her sad and pathetic choices that have led to shame and no lasting good.

Messy and needy and broken … it always seems like Jesus is closest to those people. Something about opposing the proud but giving grace to the humble (James 4:6). Maybe today that's you. And maybe today you will look around and find someone messy, needy, and broken, someone in need of Christ, and you will lay aside your bucket and instead lead him or her to Jesus through intentional questions.

Christ has the power to make dead things alive, even though the wages of our sin is death. He has the power to make us fully alive in Him so we can stop trying to get others to fill our tilted cups and instead hold them upright, that we might overflow Him to a thirsty, broken world.

Conclusion

SelfLess

In this crazy life we're living in this crazy world, it turns out that the big story isn't about us after all.

We're in each one of the scenes of our lives, true, but even those scenes aren't primarily about us. They're all a part of this bigger thing God is doing.

It's His story, and He's the star.

However, like a loving father letting his son "help" him roll out the garbage can, God invites us to be part of His story.

He graciously gives us not only a part but a *significant* part. He lets us serve Him. He lets us take part in divine encounters left and right, if we're looking for them. That means we're somehow partners with Him as He's unfolding His epic story of redemption. Are you ready to join Him?

THE MOST IMPORTANT THING

As you finish this book, let me remind you that your personal relationship with Jesus is more important than anything you have on your plate. In fact, your personal relationship with Jesus is the most important thing in your life.

So as you point your cup upward and spend time with the One who has invited you into a relationship with Himself, let me encourage you: be aggressively selfish with your personal relationship with Jesus.

Tilt your cup upward!

Where do you start? Prayer. Prayer immediately points your focus upward. Prayer immediately takes you from being merely aware of yourself to being aware of what God, the giver of life, might have for you … and then might want to do *through* you. We can't forget to pray. Spending time with God is the source of the love that we can then overflow onto others. Don't miss it.

I know many people who wonder what God is going to do about their broken families. I like to remind them that God might want to do something *through them*. Remember, you might be who God wants to use to bring love into the world. He might be using *you* to overflow to your family what they truly need, which is Him. God is in the habit of using imperfect people (and even imperfect families) for His glory. You'll know what He might have for you only if you spend the time to discern what He is saying and where He is leading.

What is God doing about [insert anything you're passionate about]? Well, it seems like He has made you pretty passionate about it. So it might be that whatever it is He wants to do about it involves you.

Spend time with God, listening. Then, when you discern His leading, respond.

God wants to use you. Now. Today. But first, tilt your cup up and receive.

If you are going to overflow to others, you must first be filled. The living water is alive and is meant to overflow through you, which is possible only after He fills you. And that takes intentional time.

Did you know the Dead Sea got its name because it has streams flowing into it but nothing coming out of it, and things can't live in that environment? It's where things go to die. We don't want to be that way. What comes into us from God is supposed to flow out to others. We must be conduits of life so we don't live dead.

God fills us so we experience true life and then outpour into others who need Him to become their Source too.

SO WHAT NOW?

If you're ready to join God in His plans, ready to have Him fill you so you can overflow to others, then start exactly where you are. That makes sense, because God won't meet you where you are not.

Set down this book and orient your cup so it's receiving from directly above. God, the source of life, will fill you with precisely what you need so you can overflow His living water to a thirsty world.

Remember God. Tilt your cup upward. Embrace your relationship with Him. When you are living in the overflow of God's life, you don't have to carry the burden of trying to be interesting—you can become interested in others. Because you will know that He is interested in you.

Try it today. Pray before you walk into a room where you will interact with people. Remember God is interested in your relationship with Him. Once you receive, overflow. Become interested in others. It's pretty revolutionary to be free from being consumed with yourself. You become selfless … self-less.

After so many years of doing it the wrong way, I finally saw how silly it is to spend so much time trying to get my cup filled by other people. It sure is ridiculous to try to work off our guilt by running up and down a hill with rocks on our backs.

But here's the great part: even the craziness of our past efforts and the tragedy of our past choices can be used to help other people. And that is significant. We may have to grab them to knock them out of their own trances, but if we can get their attention and lead them to their own encounters with Christ through intentional, loving questions, they're going to be okay.

The role we play in God's big story is not the main part, but oh, is it meaningful. Nothing is wasted. All is for His glory forever and ever, amen.